# Standing Over The Ashes

# Standing Over the Ashes

**Gather The Ruins of Your Life, Then Fertilize Your Future**

Beatrice C. Covington

Copyright © 2024 Emmanuel Jamar
All rights reserved.
ISBN-13: 979-8-9919562-0-8

## Dedication

I dedicate this book to healing!

I dedicate this book to the journey of healing. After experiencing freedom, it felt like walking beside calm waters and waking up with unexplainable joy. I now realize that most of my pain was self-inflicted, causing nearly catastrophic damage to my heart. I understand that healing is a continuous process that has no end.

# Table Of Contents

ACKNOWLEDGMENTS

INTRODUCTION

Ch 5.  PIECES OF WHAT I USED TO BE

Ch 6.  VALUE IN THE ASH

Ch 7.  WHO'S HOLDING THE MATCH

Ch 8.  NO MORE BBB (BACK-BURNER BEHAVIOR

## Healing Starts in the Middle

Ch 1.  OUTBURST OF MY SOUL

Ch 2.  FIVE ALARM BLAZE

Ch 3.  EMBERS OF THE TRUTH

Ch 4.  GOING BACK FOR WHAT'S NO LONGER THERE

ABOUT THE AUTHOR

# ~NOTE FROM THE AUTHOR~

I know the chapters of this book look like a typo. I want to reassure you that this is NOT a mistake. Chapter one of my book begins in the middle of the book. Why, might you ask? I received a revelation from God that made so much sense. True healing starts in the middle or, "the inside", and works its way to the outside. With this book being about healing, what better way to understand the process than by reading through my story and process.

## ~Covington's Thought~

Life does not have to come to a halt because of the challenges we face.
Remember that God has a purpose for every situation, even the difficult ones.
There is value in the ashes left behind after a fire.
Sometimes, it may feel like we have lost everything, but if we take the time to sift through the ashes, we will find something of value.
It is important to remember that we have not lost everything in the fire.

# ACKNOWLEDGMENTS

The gathering of these pages you are about to read would not have been possible had it not been for a synergistic outburst of the Holy Spirit through me.

- My daughters have truly been the driving force in my life since the moment I embraced my role as their mother. Each one of you—TyAnna, Whitney, Sarah, and Jordan—holds an individual spark that ignites my pride and joy. I eagerly anticipate witnessing the incredible paths that God has designed for you. Though I faced the heart-wrenching loss of your brother Emmanuel, who passed as a baby, his spirit continues to inspire us. In moments when I felt weary and tempted to give in, it was your unwavering belief in me that pushed me to strive for something extraordinary. Thank you for lifting me up and reminding me of the strength I had within! Thank you for believing in me.
- My dear granddaughters, London and Chloe, you are a beautiful reminders of God's unwavering love. I cherish you both more than words can say—more than all the bunnies in the world! And to my incredible grandsons, Ayden, Greyson, Ashton, Austin, Christian, and Quincy II, remember that you are the future leaders of our family. I am endlessly grateful to God for each one of you, and my love for you runs deep. Always hold on to your faith in God; it will guide you through life's journeys.

- To my Angelic grandson and best friend, Emmanuel (EJ), I miss you tremendously. Your incredible strength and unwavering faith have left an indelible mark on my life. Your light continues to shine as a bright light to everyone fortunate enough to have known you. Your spirit lives on in all that I do. I honor your legacy of love and faith.
- To my beloved Mother Ethel and my cherished niece Daija'~ Thank you for your relentless encouragement. Your unwavering love, support, and faith in me has been an extraordinary gift. You would think I was slacking on your life story the way you two stayed on me about completion.
- To my Sweet Mother-In-Law I want to take a moment to express my heartfelt gratitude for the incredible blessing you've given me. The gift you refer to as your son is, to me, an extraordinary man who fills my life with joy and happiness. It's clear that your love and acceptance have shaped him into the wonderful person he is today. I truly appreciate the warm embrace you've extended to me as your daughter. Our relationship is one that I deeply cherish, and I am honored to be part of your family. Thank you for everything; it means the world to me!
- To my cousin ReeRee (Marlissa), I want to take a moment to express the impact you've had on my life. When I was just 16, I found myself in a dark place, contemplating ending it all. Little do you know; you came to me in a vision and gave me hope when I needed it most. You played a pivotal role in saving my life, even if you were unaware of it at the time. Growing up, our bond as cousins and best friends was the light that guided me through many early struggles.

# ACKNOWLEDGMENTS Cont...

- To my dear cousin Christa, I reflect on all those times you've urged me to pull myself together and kept me from coming unglued. Honestly, I could fill a whole book with those moments! Your unwavering love and guidance have seen me through some of my darkest days, and I can't thank you enough for that. The bond we share as family is unbreakable, and knowing we've always got each other's backs is priceless. You have always encouraged me to be nothing less than extraordinary. After all, why would we want to be regular, right?
- To my esteemed Pastors, Ken and Beverly Jenkins, and my cherished church family at Refuge and Restoration, I want to emphasize how profoundly my life has transformed since I became part of the PROMISE. Your unwavering support, heartfelt prayers, and invaluable teachings on fully trusting in God and embracing transparency in our faith have made all the difference. I am deeply appreciative of the honesty you both embody; you have never shied away from presenting the truth as it is, without embellishment. The Word remains constant, and it's vital that we acknowledge it in its purest form, irrespective of our circumstances. Thank you for your commitment and integrity. Let's continue to walk this path of unwavering faith together.

# ACKNOWLEDGMENTS Cont...

- To my cherished circle of friends, I can't express enough how vital you have been in my life. Your pep talks and the comfort of your shoulders have been irreplaceable. I want to especially acknowledge Charmelle, Jeronica, Tamika, Kim, Sarah, Sasha, Venus, Shalanda, and Lorrie (RIP). It took me a long time to realize that my understanding of friendship often contrasted sharply with that of others around me. Throughout my journey, I've encountered individuals whose true intentions became clear only when it was too late. But you, my incredible ladies, have always been there—never hesitating to brush away my tears or answer my calls at any hour. Your dedication speaks volumes; many times, you've jumped in your cars in the dead of night to be by my side, and for that, I am forever grateful. You truly know my story, and you've respected it without ever suggesting I change a thing. Through the ups and downs, your loyalty, honesty, and embodiment of divine love have stood out. In moments when I felt like I couldn't go on, you held me up, consistently demonstrating what true friendship means. Let's continue to uplift one another and cherish the bond we've cultivated. This is the essence of friendship worth celebrating. Thank you for being my foundation.

### *To my absolutely, amazingly supportive, & phenomenal husband*

Rozelle, let me tell you why you are so incredibly important to me. You are not just my love; you are my rock, my prayer partner, and my fiercest advocate. Before you entered my life, I thought I understood what love was. But witnessing the essence of God in you revealed the true nature of love to me. You have shown me joy and demonstrated what love genuinely looks and feels like. Our daughters have also reaped the benefits of your profound influence; they have learned what love truly means, distinguishing it from the shadows of the past. You have provided them with a clear picture of what a real man embodies, allowing them to view life and love as God intended. They are free from the painful associations of abuse and mistreatment, now seeing love as a beautiful light in their lives. You pushed me to break out of my comfort zone and reminded me to focus on what truly matters to me, rather than being swayed by external pressures. You instilled in me the understanding that loving others means sometimes stepping back and letting God work in their lives. I've realized I can't save everyone, and you helped me grasp the importance of listening deeply rather than just responding. You are the reason I smile, even in my dreams. You are my source of encouragement, the poetry that flows through my heart, and the brightest star in my evening skies. Each day, you are a gift from God, one I am blessed to unwrap continuously. Your unwavering support and guidance mean everything to me. Thank you for generously sharing your world with me and enriching my life in countless ways. You are the one thing I know to be true in this ever-changing life.

# INTRODUCTION

God had given me a second book, but I hadn't quite published the first one. During that time, God spoke to me and said that the books he was giving me would bring healing to those who were searching. Although I was happy to hear this message, I didn't think much of it at the time. One day, I decided to publish the first book, but God spoke to me in a loud voice and said, "NO!" I was confused because God had given me the book, so I wondered why he didn't want me to publish it. He then told me that it was not the first book to be published and that it would be the second one in the order of how he wanted publishing to happen.

He asked me to start writing a new book that would be published first. When I inquired about the topic, he said it would be about me. I chuckled, as I had just finished writing a book about myself. He then clarified that the book would be about the fires I had faced, figuratively, and that I would have to teach people how to sift through the ashes to retrieve what is valuable. I felt a strong connection with the idea, but sometimes God doesn't reveal all the details. It's like someone enters a room with a puzzle that has twelve thousand pieces, shakes the box, and throws all the pieces up in the air. As a result, you end up with thousands of tiny pieces scattered all over the floor, and you have to put them together to create one big picture.

When I started picking up the pieces, I couldn't find anything that connected. I got frustrated and stopped looking for connections. I collected all the little pieces and put them in a box. I decided I didn't have time for it. So, I stored those pieces away.

In 2014, while I was sitting in my rocking chair on my back deck and looking at my favorite tree, I heard God say, "Do you know that if you sprinkle wood ash around the base of the tree, it acts as a repellent for insects that attempt to kill the tree? It helps the tree, Bea." I responded, "Like a fertilizer, huh?"

I held onto the idea of writing a book for a few months. One day, while taking a picture of a tree, God spoke to me and said to name the book "Standing over the Ashes", with the subtext, "Gather the ruins of your life, then fertilize your future." I immediately started writing and spent about a year working on it. However, I was often distracted and would step away from the book for months at a time before returning to it to continue writing. I even designed the cover during this time.

I thought I had finished writing my book and was ecstatic about it. I celebrated by shouting out loud that I was done. But then, I heard a voice telling me that the book wouldn't sell because the cover wouldn't attract readers. I was confused because I had chosen a perfect cover of a big tree with ashes scattered around its base. However, the voice insisted that the cover wouldn't make sense to anyone but me. So, I went back to the drawing board and came up with a new cover that would make readers pick up my book. The new cover featured a man standing in front of a burning fire, and it spoke volumes.

Full of excitement because he had approved, I screamed again, "Yazzzzzzzz! I'm done!" Unbeknownst to me, God said, "No, you are not." I was now angry. "What do you mean? I know I'm done!" He said, "No, you are not."

It was then that he reminded me of his desire for my book to bring healing to the readers. He reminded me, "It would be catastrophic if everyone else got healed except for you." He advised me to deal with more of my personal issues.
I was taken aback because I believed that I had poured my heart out onto the pages, just as he had asked me to do. I told him that I didn't understand what he meant. He then explained that I still had unresolved issues to deal with. I asked, "What issues have I not dealt with?" I felt like I had disclosed more than enough.

He told me that I would never truly heal if I continued to hide behind a facade. I was protective of everyone, and I didn't want to tell every story, although it was my story from my point of view. It wasn't until the summer of 2021 that I was finally ready to pursue my own personal healing. This journey finally brought me to completion, but it had to start in the middle.

# Go To the Center of the Book for *Chapter 1*

# Chapter 5

PIECES OF WHAT I USED TO BE

## The Crying Tree

I came upon a crying tree,
Then ask the tree why must you weep.

The tree looked down and said to me,
He swept me off my feet.

Well please don't cry was my reply,
I know how you must feel.

Love can hurt and never heal,
But you must know when it is real.

Then a leaf fell from the tree,
Like tears dropping to the ground.

I felt its pain and bowed my head,
Then suddenly looked around.

That leaf that fell was my heart,
You were the wind from the very start.

But until you know and come to me,
I'll be trapped and fallen never free.

**(Spoken Words 2007)**

## PIECES OF WHAT I USED TO BE

The iconic phrase, "Mirror, mirror on the wall, who's the fairest of them all?" from the tale of Snow White resonates with many of us. Yet, how often do we pause in front of a mirror before stepping out of our homes? Most people do this ritual. We rely on mirrors for everything from styling our hair to washing our faces and brushing our teeth. Applying makeup without a mirror seems nearly impossible. Just think about attempting to shape your eyebrows without any reflection or image to guide you. Clearly, mirrors have become indispensable in our everyday lives.

We take another glance in the mirror to ensure our hair is neat, our clothes fit well, and our teeth are clean before engaging with others. This habit helps us avoid potential embarrassment, like discovering an unsightly detail that could detract from our confidence. However, we must confront the falsehoods that mirrors can convey. These deceptive reflections can dominate our thoughts, shaping our self-image and influencing how we believe the world perceives us. If you've ever felt misled by your own reflection, you understand the emotional toll it can take.

Even now, I sometimes see a distorted version of myself. But what's more troubling than being misled is the daily return to the same painful narrative, expecting a different result. Approaching the mirror by the front door, I hoped to see a new version of myself. Yet, my reality remained unchanged from the day before. Have you ever gazed into your own eyes and accepted the same image repeatedly? Perhaps you, too, yearn for a different perception or feeling. The issue may not solely lie in your present situation; it could be the lingering shadows of past experiences that keep you tethered, making the mirror echo, "YOU ARE STILL that broken, abandoned, rejected, unworthy, unloved, lonely individual!" It's the mirror you choose to keep. It's the reflection you continuously face!

This mirror was crafted to reveal the present, not the past. While it may seem like an ordinary mirror, it harbors a sinister essence within its frame. What appears to be an unblemished sheet of glass is, in reality, a shattered reflection hanging on the wall. You might feel perplexed right now but allow me to clarify why I refer to this mirror as shattered. When you gaze into it, all you perceive is your current state, not the person staring back at you. What you see is the anguish and turmoil you've endured. You've become so familiar with your brokenness that it's all that registers. Stand before it once more and declare, "Mirror, mirror on the wall!"

For years, I stood before this mirror, witnessing the same reflection day in and day out. Even when positive changes occurred, I remained blind to my own transformation, still viewing my life through the fragments of that broken glass. This mindset left me feeling incomplete and unworthy. How can you mend what you cannot even recognize? You've trained yourself to perceive the distorted image in the mirror, which reflects your inner struggles rather than your true self.

Open your eyes and take a moment to observe your surroundings. What aspects of your life, both external and internal, are in disarray? To transform your world, you must first shift your mindset, and that begins with removing the mirror that reflects your past. Tear it down! For too long, you've been trapped in a cycle of destructive thoughts and behaviors, living out a distorted image of yourself shaped by past experiences. Letting go of that negative self-perception is crucial.

Steer clear of the valley of shattered mirrors; they only serve to keep you feeling fragmented and immobilized. The choice is in your hands! You can either continue to view yourself in pieces or opt to hang a new mirror that reflects your true self. It may seem unconventional, but it's essential if you wish to see yourself as God sees you—whole, complete, and healed.

While you cannot change your past, you can certainly learn from it. Your experiences do not have to dictate who you are. Instead, channel that energy into creating something positive. By accepting your circumstances, you can begin to manage the emotional turmoil and integrate it into your life.

Reflecting on my own journey, I remember the fragments of who I once was. In Seattle, I endured domestic violence, waking up each day in a battle for my life, filled with fear not just for myself but for my daughter as well. I felt weak, allowing myself to be disrespected, abused, and isolated. But it wasn't a reflection of my worth; it stemmed from the choices I made in my relationships. The pivotal moment came when I chose to embrace God, which empowered me to make the decision to leave that toxic situation behind.

The core issue lies in the necessity for greater ownership in our lives. We must take responsibility for the challenges we face. Often, we shy away from the tougher choices because they seem daunting, opting instead for the easier path, which can ultimately lead to our downfall. By embracing our mistakes, decisions, and experiences, we can liberate ourselves to identify our recurring patterns, allowing us to avoid those detrimental routes in the future. Remember, we are not bound to those paths, alternatives exist. Even if we find ourselves on that road again, there are always detours available to guide us back to our true direction.

I won't pretend that I haven't traveled that same road multiple times. However, I eventually had to confront the question of why I kept returning. My mind was so cluttered with distractions that I failed to notice the guidance being offered to me. We must learn to eliminate the distractions that drain our energy and hinder our ability to hear that quiet, guiding voice when we are being steered toward a better path.

Have you ever questioned why you feel unwell, overwhelmed, or downcast while grappling with health challenges? It could be that you are suppressing your pain. Let go of the guilt that tells you it's your fault and embrace the freedom that comes from understanding that life continues beyond the flames. It's time to change your viewpoint! Seek the lessons hidden within your experiences and take a moment for self-reflection. Who are you really? I assure you; this new perspective will unveil insights that can transform your understanding of yourself. Witness the remarkable changes in your life as your perspective shifts.

We often find ourselves so eager for love that we overlook the red flags right in front of us. It's not that we don't see them; rather, we choose to turn a blind eye. It's crucial to break this cycle. You are worthy of experiencing the profound beauty of divine love. I once thought that suffering was an unavoidable aspect of love, but I've come to understand that it should be a source of joy and happiness that uplifts your spirit. If there is any pain, it should stem from the fear of losing that love once it is found.
I have faced the challenge of being in a toxic relationship myself. Deep down, I recognized that I was entangled with someone harmful, yet I lacked the strength to walk away initially. I kept rationalizing their actions, convinced that I could change them. The truth is, we cannot change others. In our attempts to bring positivity into their lives, we often end up creating chaos in our own. Living a lie amidst turmoil is akin to being engulfed in flames.

It's time to liberate yourself and embrace the truth. You have come to terms with the harsh reality of your past experiences. Now, as you reflect on your life, you may realize that you feel incomplete. Some parts of you were lost in the turmoil, and you are still on a quest to fill that emptiness. However, this should not be seen as a negative. Often, we must endure challenging times to emerge stronger and more refined. Acknowledge this truth. The old has been cleared away to allow the new to flourish.

Why do we hesitate to examine our lives and evaluate our current state? By dedicating time to reflect on our actions and traits, we can learn from our past mistakes and prevent repeating them. It's a straightforward principle of growth through experience. As the wise often say, it's all about confronting and learning from your missteps.

If all unresolved situations were dreams, it would feel like déjà vu. You experience the same lighting, smells, and surroundings that you can identify with. You might say to yourself, "I've been here before. Why does this feel like something I've done before or someone I've been with before?" The answer is simple - the person you're dealing with is just like those from your past, and you're on the same road again. You must recognize that you have been here before and identify how you got here. If you don't take inventory of your past, you end up with another similar situation. The circumstances are familiar, even if the people are different.

You don't have to create a new story. There comes a time in your life when you won't even have to tell the story. It won't even matter. At least it won't matter to the person who wants to love you. You won't have to itemize your pain or experiences. They will love you through the pain and accept the pieces of you that still exist. It will be those pieces that are so delicately put back together, which would make you see the beauty in the picture when you allow someone into the little dark corner of your universe. They begin to sit patiently with you as you sift through your own ashes. They find the valuable parts of you that you thought had been lost in the fiery furnace of your previous hell. It is amazing when you're approaching the trash can with the shovelful of ashes of your life, and that one person comes up to stop you at the dumpsite to show you the smile you almost lost at the landfill; you are so damaged that you did not see the value of you, hidden in a pile of debris.

There is value in who you are and what you have endured. Stop claiming broken, angry, flustered, scorned, and even alright. It's not alright to not want to put the puzzle together again. Do you realize there is still a beautiful image in a puzzle with 12 missing pieces? It's not about who you used to be but rather who you are presently and who you are being made and molded into for your future.

I used to be afraid and critical of myself. I struggled with insecurity until I was about 39 years old. I didn't know how to love myself, so how could I guide or correct someone else about how they loved me? As I learned how to love myself, my identity began to transform. I became fearless, happy, and aware of my feelings enough to speak up when something didn't feel right. You can't move forward in the tangles of who you used to be. The keyword *used to be*. There is no future in the past, so use the remnants of it to fuel your future.

Keep asking yourself this question as you move into your life assessment:Who am I? If you cannot immediately define who you are, you don't know yourself. It's not the end of the world, but knowing who you are is your most valuable weapon in life outside of GOD. You can't help yourself if you have not met that AMAZING person trapped in the skin you wear daily.

Let's try answering the question.

Close your eyes for a minute and say WHO AM I?

Now, don't ramble off the normal, obvious things about you and your life. Try to stay away from the textbook responses of I'm a daughter or son, a husband or a wife, a teacher or an accountant, a mother or a father. That's obvious to even a hacker who has access to your social media, email, or text. Those things do not identify who you are. If you were no longer an accountant, would you still be you? If you were not a father any longer, would you still be you? If you were no longer a husband or a wife, would you still be you? So, who are you? That is the question!

Don't diminish who GOD has called you to be. He did not create a shallow and vague version of you. He created you fearfully and wonderfully (Psalm 139:14).

But answering the question of who you are answers and uncovers the passion that makes you who you are. What drives you? What defines you? What special skill sets do you have? What are your core values? What is your personality like, and what do you believe in? What would you do for free simply because it makes your heart sing?

Now, look at your answers to those questions. They will help you identify who you are, not who the world or your family says you are. You don't have to be or do what people want you to be or do. Now again, who are you? Get to know that person and be that person every day.

You can confidently and clearly answer that question without hesitation: Who am I? It's not enough to write out who you are but feel and know it in your heart so the next time you're asked, you will never shrug your shoulders and say well, I am this, and I am that. You will hold your head high, shoulders back, and chest out and say I am! Even God said I am who I am. (Exodus 3:14) KNOW WHO YOU ARE.

Life teaches you to hide who you are. So, we then limit ourselves and our response to what our roles and labels are in life versus identifying who we are. Dim your shine for No One!

Now that you know who you are, you must cease the idea of staying stuck in the past. You are no longer going to allow it to define you. You will stop leaving the past unresolved. Address it all, no matter how bad it is. It's a pain that cannot be ignored unless you truly just love this place. Don't get me wrong; many people are okay with it because they have sat in that mess for so long that it has become a comfort zone of PAIN. Though it hurts, it feels GOOD. How crazy is that? You'd rather sit there because it's familiar. NOOOOOO!

If you leave it the way it is, it will continue to vex you with sorrow, pain, and anger. You must be willing to accept that you cannot change the past and what has happened to you, but you have a choice to change your future and how you move forward in this life. God allowed you to be here in this place and in this season for a reason. Don't walk around defeated when you can walk around on purpose.

YOU HAVE TO take that long walk backward to heal forward. You cannot heal what you cannot see. FACE that thing and take back control by not holding on to it but forgiving it and purging it completely. Be okay with SCREAMING AND CRYING. You walked around with a weight you didn't have to carry! You have trusted yourself and that box in which you kept all those secrets and pains. I dare you to trust all of it to God. It's simple: go to the closet, pick the box up, walk it right up to Jesus, and lay it all at his feet. Then walk away! Head High, Shoulders Back, and Chest Out.

No one is asking you to dismiss the facts, but you can surely view it through a different lens. When I took my shades off and put on my glasses, I could see CLEARLY. I was able to see with a forgiving eye versus a victimized eye. I was able to see that the abuser was abused, and maybe no one knew their story. When I began seeing things differently, it opened my heart to forgiveness. My pain became purpose and passion. The temporary inconvenience was for permanent improvement. At my lowest, I heard God say to me to lift up my head and stop seeing things as REJECTION WHEN HE WAS PROTECTING ME FOR REDIRECTION!

You must hit the reset to create the future you were supposed to have. Your life is like a roll of film; before the images/negatives can be developed, the photographer must put them through a period of processing. That's the same thing God is doing. He takes one unclear image after the next, and he puts it through a chemical process in a DARK room. He hangs up one image, followed by the next as it emerges from the developing phase. You still can't see the clear image until it's fully dry and comes out of that room. This is LIFE… Trust the process. Trust that even though you don't see the final picture, God knows what it looks like. Stop opening that dang door before the image is ready to be seen. WE mess things up by rushing to be nosey instead of trusting the one shooting the images in the first place.

The picture you keep looking at is a piece of who you USE TO BE!
Will you trust the Master for your next images?

# Chapter 6

## VALUE IN THE ASH

## ~6~
## VALUE IN THE ASH

Have you ever heard of the idiom "Don't throw the baby out with the bathwater?" It's an expression used to convey that one should not discard or reject an entire thing, idea, concept, practice, or project just because there are some negative aspects to it. Instead, one should identify and keep the positive aspects of it while discarding the negative ones. The baby, in this sense, represents the good part that can be preserved, while the bathwater, on the other hand, is often dirty after the baby is washed and must be discarded. Similarly, the bad or useless aspects of a concept should be discarded, much like bathwater, while the good parts should be retained, like the baby.

Likewise, get rid of the ashes in your life, not the valuables you can find as you search through the remains of your situation.
I believe it is important for us to come back to this place on our journey. In the beginning, it may be difficult to process the devastation and the pain we feel. However, as time passes and we begin to sort through what remains of our world, revisiting this site will allow us to reflect on what we lost and how it happened. This reflection is a critical step in our healing process.

Often, when faced with the task of rebuilding, our instinct is to pick up our shovels and begin cleaning up the mess. However, this can be problematic as our shovels may be branded with labels that reflect our current situations and mindsets. I won't discuss your shovel, but I will share some of the shovels that I've encountered.

I was left with negative feelings attached to the ash, but the fires that had triggered them were attempting to define my identity. It's crucial to acknowledge both who you are and who you are not. Find the strength to speak against those things.

If you constantly engage in negative self-talk, the things you allow others to say about you and the things you say to yourself will eventually become a reality in your life. Often, we tend to replay the things that people say about us in our minds repeatedly, almost as if we are learning lines for a role in a TV show. This process can become so ingrained that we start to identify with these negative labels and thoughts as part of our identity. Negative self-talk acts as an accelerant that fuels the fire of negative thinking, causing it to spread more quickly and easily.

Taking care of ourselves and our surroundings is closely linked to how we speak to or about ourselves. If we do not cherish and love ourselves, how can we expect someone else to do it?

Let's consider some examples of everyday life. How do we maintain our living spaces, whether it is a house, an apartment, or just a room that we occupy? Similarly, how do we care for our cars if we own one? These possessions reflect what we value and represent an extension of ourselves. What about the clothes we wear? Do we throw them on the floor or take care of them properly by separating them based on fabrics, colors, washing instructions, and wet vs dry?
Neglecting these small details could affect our mood and energy levels. Making our bed every morning, not leaving dirty dishes for weeks, and following a routine help in maintaining a sense of order in our lives. We may have taken many of these things for granted, but they are crucial for our self-care.

When my husband and I purchased our first home together, I must admit that after many years, I became ungrateful because I wanted some updates. My husband had previously discussed the possibility of expanding the house to give me the bedroom I wanted. Unfortunately, my negative energy was reflected in my home and how I felt about it. I wasn't being fair to my husband; although my actions may have been silent, my negative energy was very loud.

I stopped caring for our home. I started letting the mail pile up on the dining room table, boxes of random things sat untouched in corners of the room, and my clothes piled up on the Peloton. At one point, my husband made a joke about the Peloton being an expensive clothes hanger, but I could tell he was upset. I had been neglecting our home, and it was hurting him, even though he hadn't said anything about it. I had complained so much about not having the things I wanted in our home that it had become disrespectful.

I noticed that my lack of self-love was affecting our home, and I was passing that negative energy onto my husband. I realized that my behavior was unfair to him, and he did not deserve to be treated that way.

I made the mistake of thinking that if I started fixing the house, I would start loving it again. However, I now understand that my actions were sending the message that I did not appreciate how hard my husband worked to provide for us.

After painting the walls, I purchased oversized artwork for each room and a beautiful master bedroom set. To complete the look, I added oversized rugs to cover the carpet that I previously disliked. I also painted the entire house, which looked like a colorful, chaotic mess. My husband was taken aback when he came home every day to see walls that were once white now resembled the aftermath of a grandchild's paint party. I even painted the light fixtures, heating and air conditioning vents, and several baseboards. Though he never hurt my feelings, he often joked, asking who the contractor was and if we could get our money back.

Wait, did I mention that our bedroom is approximately 12 feet by 10 feet? I purchased an entire bedroom set for it, including a king-sized bed with a headboard and footboard, a dresser with a mirror, a large armoire with double doors, two oversized nightstands, and a storage bench.

It took a whole year for my furniture to arrive due to import and export challenges caused by COVID-19. There were multiple shipment delays, which resulted in the furniture arriving on our anniversary. I was overjoyed to receive it, but my husband was not initially impressed. He had never seen the furniture before and was surprised to find out that I had purchased more than what could fit in our room. The only items that could fit were the king-sized bed and one nightstand.

My husband made a joke, saying, "Woman! Did you not think this through?" I replied quickly that I did, but only after the fact. I suggested that we use our daughter Sarah's old room as a dressing room since it was right next to ours. However, setting up and moving all the furniture into the home took forever due to its size and weight. Zell had to grab his tools and help the young men set up the bed because they were facing some challenges. Unfortunately, the delivery ruined the anniversary plans he had made for us. Our reservation was at 7 PM, but they were still setting up a few minutes into the 7 o'clock hour. My husband had made plans, and I messed it up.

The result of our anniversary was that my husband said he loved the furniture. He spent time loading his drawers with clothes and organizing cologne on top of his armoire. I was smiling from ear to ear because it looked amazing, even in two rooms. The oversized rugs gave a new flare to each space and to the home. I felt re-energized and said, "Lord, I love this house! It feels and looks so beautiful." I began to care again about our home and operated at a higher level of gratitude. I also noticed that I started treating myself and the things God had blessed me with better.

---

I've come to realize that everything I have, including myself, is a precious gift from God. With this understanding, I've started to treat myself and everything around me with more respect and gratitude. Every day, I remind myself that these are gifts to be cherished, and I feel more fulfilled and content than ever before.

After I corrected my heart and mindset and became a grateful wife again, things began to shift very quickly. It was just one month later when my husband, Zell, saw pictures of a house coming to the real estate market. He suggested we put an offer on the home. I laughed inside because I thought he was joking. After all, we had not been actively looking for a new home. A few years earlier, we had house-shopped but stopped when we couldn't find what made our hearts sing. A day or two passed, and he asked what the lender said. I realized he was serious and immediately contacted the lender.

We received approval to purchase our new home, and 30 days later, we signed the final documents. During that period, I found myself crying and packing repeatedly as I struggled to accept that we were leaving the home I had grown to love again. I began to pray and realized that we could have moved earlier, but my lack of gratitude had held us back.

I didn't see it as punishment, but I was reminded of a scripture that says, "to whom much is given, much is required." I understood that if we were faithful with a little, we would be blessed with more. Furthermore, I thought about the children of Israel who took 40 years to reach the promised land due to their disobedience, ungratefulness, and disbelief in God's promises.

I connected to this story because my husband has always loved me properly. He is an amazing provider and would give me the world on a silver platter every day of my life. If I ask for the moon, he will find a way to get to the moon and bring it back to me. God gave my husband a vision of another home that would fulfill most of our requirements, and it was waiting for us. However, I had to learn the virtues of patience and gratitude. At the time, I did not love myself properly, so I looked for love in the material surroundings of my home.

Tomorrow, you'll be walking up to your life with a shovel and beginning to discard everything without thought; many will not think twice about taking time to sift through the ashes.
I want to remind you of something. When you look at your shovels, what do you see? Perhaps you're having trouble finding it because of the ash. But, my dear, you should drop the shovel and sift for the valuable things that remain - joy, healing, restoration, redemption, love, purification, refinement, and so much more. Don't miss out on the promise of finding something good amidst the pain.

It's important to realize that the choices we make have consequences. However, even in the aftermath, there is still value to be found. We made those choices willingly, even though we might have had the option to walk away. Perhaps, at the time, we weren't strong enough, or maybe we believed that change would come eventually.

I often hear people say that they don't have time to deal with their problems and instead choose to ignore them. However, it's important to understand that these problems belong exclusively to them. It's the ash of their very own existence, their choices, their afflictions, and their generational curses that no one wants to deal with. Simply put, it's their own mess to deal with. Having the mindset of not wanting to face it says that they like being in this place of pain. Some people are comfortable with being there because they have been in that place for so long that leaving it scares them. They enjoy pity parties.

People tolerate you, but not for long. It's an energy that keeps pushing people away. They're tired of picking up balloons and streamers at Party City every time they see you. The pity party needs to stop. It can be emotionally draining. This isn't Painting with a Twist! People around you no longer want to get the paint and canvas to see the story like you do. DEAL with your fires to find the good parts of who God said you are.

Don't try to rebuild the same life after a tragedy! Instead, take this opportunity to learn from the experience and find the good in the ashes. Create a new home for yourself and establish a pattern of making better choices that will bring you peace. It's important to remember that life will always have challenges and difficulties, but not every problem will be a significant crisis. By learning how to handle more minor issues, you will be better prepared to deal with more significant challenges in the future.

With each new challenge, you will gain more knowledge and experience and be able to handle it more efficiently. The key is to be proactive and address any problems before they become too big. By doing this, you can put out the flames with an extinguisher rather than call the entire fire department. Remember, every experience is an opportunity to learn and grow, and with each challenge, you will gain more value and become better equipped to handle whatever comes your way.

Take some time to evaluate yourself and your life. If you don't, you risk losing more than material possessions and hurting people's feelings. You may also lose your sanity after the problems you've avoided. I'm speaking from personal experience on many levels, and I want to emphasize this point: it sneaks up on you!

Sometimes, the issue may seem small and manageable, but if you keep avoiding it, it can eventually become the one thing that destroys everything. I know from experience that pain can be all-consuming and have a universal language. Many of life's problems can be managed, but it's up to you to decide how big or small they are.

But if you ignore it, the fire will consume you, your thoughts, and everything around you. This kind of fire tears families apart. No one noticed the smoke, warning signs, or subtle messages. Nobody noticed the shift in behavior or the fire burning behind your eyes. We find value when we survive the blaze. Your life doesn't have to be a recurring blaze after the next. Let me give you an example of how I found, or rather, how God exposed some value in ashes of nearly 30 years of life.

When I was around nine years old, my sister and I used to walk up to the local corner store every Sunday morning, regardless of the weather, to buy the Sunday paper for my mother. She was interested in finding the sales and coupons, usually in the middle of the paper. On the other hand, I was excited to read the comics while my stepdad was looking for the TV guide.

The store was called the Jamaican Food Shop, and it was situated in my neighborhood, about a block away from my house. The store owner, George, was a well-known older Jamaican man who was very friendly and nice. He had a very thick Jamaican accent, sometimes making it difficult for me to understand him. I often just nodded my head and said yes sir or no sir because of this. However, he pointed out a lot while speaking, which helped me to follow along with his conversation.

George was a familiar face in the neighborhood, and we all trusted him because his store had been there for a long time. He had watched us grow up. One day, while I was in the store, I mentioned that I wanted to buy a birthday card for my mom. George took me to the tall and thin card holder near the window at the entrance. He asked me if I knew how much money I would need to buy the card, and I replied that I didn't know.

As he spun the card rack around, we looked at many cards. He asked me, "Do you see anything that catches your attention?" I shook my head and replied, "No sir, not yet." However, every time we came across a card that I thought I might like, I pointed and asked, "What about this one?" He would take the card up to his face, look over the glasses that sat on the tip of his nose, and either read the card or immediately reject the selection if it was a sympathy or congratulations card. The birthday cards he found were unappealing to me, and I would indicate to him with my facial expression that I didn't like them.

We were going through some cards and having a good laugh when I pointed to a particularly pretty one and asked Mr. George what it was. I noticed a certain expression on his face when he opened the card that made me think it wouldn't work. When I asked him about it, he simply replied with a thick accent, "Noooooo." I felt a bit sad because we had gone through almost all the cards at this point. However, Mr. George eventually explained that the card I had pointed to was one of the blank ones without any words on it.

I was very happy when he said that. I looked at him and replied, "Well, Mr. George, that's perfect!" I can write my own words on the beautiful card. We both smiled because I had found the card I would buy from him in a few weeks. He told me that it was priced at 15 cents. I thanked him and now had an idea of how much I would need to save to purchase the card.

Week after week, I would visit the store to buy my mom's Sunday paper. Each time, I'd sneak a glance at a specific card, hoping that nobody else had bought it. Sometimes, I would even take the card and hide it behind others so that it wouldn't be seen. Finally, the day arrived for my mom's 30th birthday. When I walked into the store that morning, the excitement was evident on my face. I had such a big smile that I think Mr. George could see all my back teeth. He noticed my enthusiasm and immediately walked out from behind the counter to join me at the card rack. We found the card we had hidden weeks earlier for this special day. After that, we picked up the Sunday paper, making sure to keep all the coupons and the TV guide intact. This was the only reason I came every Sunday morning. I paid for my mom's newspaper first, and then Mr. George placed the paper in a plastic grocery bag to ensure it wouldn't fall out or get damaged.

After securing Mom's paper, I paid fifteen cents for the card which he placed it in a very thin brown paper bag. I was overjoyed and left the store feeling excited. I had never written a card before, so this was a new experience for me. I was looking forward to customizing the card specifically for my mom. No other mom would have the same card as mine.

When I arrived home, I immediately gave my mom her newspaper and then rushed to my room. I sat on my bed with my card, a pen, and a hardback book that I used as a sturdy surface. I didn't even think about it; I just opened the card and started writing my heart out on the cardstock, using the pen to guide my words. It felt so natural, and I remember my words feeling bigger than life. I was absolutely certain that my mom would not only be surprised but also appreciate it because of the thought that I put into it. I could have easily bought myself some penny candy, cookies, a Chick-O stick, some Mike & Ike's, or even a pickle but I wanted my mother to be delighted that I got her something for her birthday.

After I was done writing, I got off my bed and put the card into its envelope, but I didn't want to lick the back to seal it. The thought of how many people, including George, had touched the card and all the envelopes grossed me out. So, I skipped the licking part and went to my mom's room with my
hands behind my back, shouting, "MOM!!!!!!! I've got something for you." I felt proud to give her the card, and my heart still warms when I remember that moment. As I walked into her room, I whipped the card from behind my back and wished my mom a happy birthday.

Now, the moment I had been waiting for had arrived. I gave my mom a card and anxiously waited for her response. She opened the card and read it carefully. I was standing next to her bed, and I couldn't help but feel excited. Suddenly, she looked up at me and said, "Awwwwwww, that was so sweet!" I was overjoyed! She loved it, and I couldn't have been happier.

But just as quickly as her kind words had come, they were gone. The card flipped over in her hand in what felt like slow motion. She looked at the back of the card, and her expression changed. The words that followed crushed my spirit.

Looking up at me, she said, "15 cents!!!! Is that all I'm worth to you?" I felt like I was in a Spike Lee production, moving slowly on the screen with a dumb, puppy-dog half-smirk on my face. My smile had been crushed, and I felt terrible.

Before I continue with the story, I want to clarify something. Although my mother said those words, I don't think she realized how deeply they impacted my life. She was never a cruel mother who would intentionally hurt her children. She probably meant it as a joke, but as a child, I didn't understand sarcasm and took her words to heart. I managed to hold back my tears and put on a brave face as I left the room, but inside, I felt shattered.

As soon as I reached my room, I closed the door and went over to my bookshelf, where all my music and systems were. I knelt down, turned on the music on my record player, and tried to put the pieces of myself back together. I lay down on the floor next to the record player and silently cried for hours. The only thing that played in my mind was, "Is that all I'm worth to you? Fifteen cents?"
I cried so hard in secret, sobbing uncontrollably. I tried to stifle my tears, but they continued to flow out of me like a waterfall. The pain and heartache I felt were unbearable, and my body seemed to shut down. At that moment, I believe I even forgot to breathe.

As I reflect on the past, I realize that it was probably the first time I experienced a broken heart, and the person who caused it didn't even know it. In hindsight, I have come to understand that we, as parents, can unintentionally harm our children without even realizing it.

After my mom's birthday, I found myself going through the motions of life with a fake smile plastered on my face. I kept replaying the moment when she asked, "Is that all I'm worth, 15 cents?"

My mom's birthday falls close to Mother's Day, so I made a personal promise to myself that I would always give her the best. From that day on, everything I did had to be larger than life and exceptionally amazing. I was determined to make sure that anything I gave her would be something she would love, adore, and cherish for the rest of her life.

Four years after I gave my mom that card, I landed my very first job. It was a time when most people were making minimum wage, around $3.15 per hour. However, I was making more than twice that amount, at about $7.50 per hour. You might be curious as to how a 13-year-old could be making that much money. Well, let me explain. My Aunt Willie Ellen was the manager of housekeeping at a local hotel in Missouri and she urgently needed help during the summer.

One early summer morning, her entire staff was full of complaints and was providing poor service to the establishment. She was over all the excuses, call-offs, and no-shows. She had over 100 rooms that had to be cleaned, but her staff was going against the grain of her leadership. She criticized these adults for their laziness and lack of professionalism and told them that even a child could follow these simple instructions and get this work done in a faster and more efficient way than they had been operating.

The group of women laughed at my aunt and told her they were not concerned about being fired because she needed them. This made my aunt angry, and she impulsively fired nine housekeepers, keeping only the two who worked efficiently and without complaint. After firing them, my aunt panicked and wondered what she would do without her staff. Her husband suggested she call her nieces to help out during the summer in exchange for payment, which would help us with our school expenses. We agreed. Who would have thought the skills of this first job would be a part of the shovel that would later assist in digging me out of the ashes of yet another fire I would find myself in.

When we first arrived at the establishment, we worked so hard that the owners asked if we could continue working for them during the summer and on weekends when we returned to school. It was quite an achievement for us to have a job at the ages of 13 and 15. Initially, the pay was at the minimum wage, but before the summer ended, we made over seven dollars per hour. One of the owners seemed to have taken a liking to me, and he would occasionally make comments and smile at me. He even gave me big teddy bears and offered to buy my school supplies, but he never tried anything inappropriate. However, his girlfriend was so upset that she flew back to her country for several weeks.

I share my hotel experience to explain how I was earning a lot of money. Only later did I realize I was making more than my mother. However, I don't think she ever knew about it. She never asked me how much I made because I could provide for myself and shower her with gifts. It made me happy to think I could give her things I thought she wanted, liked, or needed.

I believe my efforts to please my mother led to me becoming a people-pleaser at any cost. Unfortunately, this habit spilled over into my friendships, workplace, and romantic relationships with my partners. For over 30 years of my life, I poured my time, attention, and love into people who didn't deserve it. This became a part of who I was, and I struggled to break free from this pattern of behavior. Although, my mom's words seemed small, it was smoke that was brewing into a full blown fire.

Despite that pain, I picked up a blessing. I became a stronger writer through the many challenges I faced on my journey. Writing and music became my therapy. I could take your words and transfer them onto 23 blank lines to create a masterpiece as if I had taken a paintbrush to a canvas.

# Chapter 7

## WHO'S HOLDING THE MATCH?

## ~7~
## WHO'S HOLDING THE MATCH?

Now that the smoke has cleared, I want to welcome you back to parts of your life you may have forgotten. As we stand here and look around, we can see that not everything was destroyed. Some things had to be burned up in the fire, but some things survived.

You can clean up and bring back some of the things to a usable condition. I've mentioned before that there is value in your life and every situation. We shouldn't act as if everything is destroyed; it's lazy not to take the time to see what's left. It's natural to have strong emotions as you go through the remnants. Is there anything you can salvage? Take this opportunity to purge anything that should've been destroyed.

While you're assessing the situation, look at yourself and ask, "Who did I give access to?" If it wasn't me who caused the series of catastrophic events, then the question is, who did?

Even though someone else might have been responsible for starting the fire, you still have to take ownership for giving them the means to do so.
It's time to recognize how valuable you and your life are to others. There's always someone watching and hoping that you'll make it so they can, too. But if you keep being careless with your life and what God has given, you'll find out that not only did you take yourself down in the fire, but you also took other people down who could've survived if they hadn't been watching you.

Stop giving everyone and everything access to you! Ask yourself, "Who is holding the match?" If you are a parent, your children are watching! Is that not significant to you?

Who is holding the match?

Recently, I had a conversation with someone about the challenges she was facing in her life. She had been through a terrifying experience that could have ended her life. Her family and friends were scared and felt helpless during this difficult time. It's incredibly stressful to feel so helpless and unable to resolve something that is weighing heavily on your heart.

I suggested that she reflect on the times when she felt protected and provided for by a higher power. I encouraged her to recognize the undeniable presence of God in her life during times of trouble. I reminded her of the importance of gratitude and urged her to reflect on her choices to avoid similar situations in the future.

I also conveyed the idea that she played a part in what happened to her. I explained that there are often warning signs before a crisis, and it's important to pay attention to the connections we make and the choices we align ourselves with. It may seem insensitive to imply that it was her fault, but sometimes we contribute to our own problems. We can't make positive changes if we refuse to face our truths.

Ultimately, no matter how much we talk, the person on the receiving end may not truly hear what we're saying. The delusion of it all is what breaks my heart. All I want to do is shake people and say, "WAKE UP!" The Devil almost had you, and you keep missing the fact that a rope fell from out of nowhere and pulled you to safety.

What will it take to open your eyes and see that many of the fires in your life have started because of a contribution? Who did you give access to? Who did you give the power to? Holding the match could signify control over a volatile situation. Could the fire be a consequence?

Not everything in your life may have fallen apart due to external factors. Even if it did, there's a good chance that you played a significant role in it as well. Take a moment to reflect and ask yourself, who held the match that started the fire? Or better yet, who gave the match to the person who lit the fire?

It's important to understand that fire possesses many properties that can be either beneficial or harmful, depending on how it's utilized. When used properly, fire can provide warmth and protection. However, when misused, it can lead to destruction and chaos. Similarly, when we face the challenges of life, the experiences we encounter can either help us grow or break us down. It's easy to blame others for our problems and avoid taking responsibility.

However, reflecting on our actions can help us become better individuals. Instead of fixating on what we cannot change, we should focus on what we can control and address, identify our roles, and establish measures to prevent similar situations from occurring. Life is unpredictable. Things will fall apart just as they will grow and be built.

It's possible that you were not solely responsible for certain events, but even then, there is still accountability in how you allowed yourself to live and feel because of what someone did to you. If there was a time when you stopped moving, stopped growing, and stopped believing, then you gave that person power over you. Even after they were gone, the lingering effects of their actions continued to impact your life. It's time to reclaim your power!

There's a story in the Bible in John 5:6 where Jesus encountered a man lying near the pool of Bethesda. The man had been sick for years. Jesus asked him, "Do you WANT to be healed?" This might seem like an odd question, considering the man's condition and the fact that he was near a place known for healing. However, the question was important then and is still relevant today for those who are suffering. God will never force himself on you.

You have to want to receive what he has for you. You have been given free will, so when he asks, "Do you want to be healed?" or "Do you want to be free?" your response and heart posture determine whether things will change.

Imagine if the man lying there had said, "No, I'm good. I'm just hanging out here with my friends, watching others." Even though Jesus knew the man wanted to be healed, he had to ask for it. This showed self-awareness in his response, taking ownership and control instead of blaming others. When he answered Jesus with a "YES, I want to be made well," Jesus gave him instructions to "STAND UP AND WALK."

Some people choose to stay in their current condition because it's familiar and comfortable. They fear being free because it comes with the responsibility of not returning to the place or thing they were healed from. It's sad that many people won't face their challenges and instead choose to stay stuck, blaming others for the life they didn't achieve. I want to emphasize that sometimes things go wrong in our lives, and it's not necessarily because of our performance, behavior, knowledge, or ability to perform. The hardest part has always been protecting myself from repeat cycles. I've questioned myself many times: what's wrong with me? Had my friend been right about me giving too much control to others?

After I divorced my children's dad, I met a guy at an event through a mutual connection. He and I became extremely close, but not in the way you may think. We shared many vulnerable moments but never had to make it sexual. He had a genuine love for me as a friend. There were moments when we had to contain the emotional side of our friendship because there was intense attraction on both sides. Most of our time spent together was authentic healing and conversations.

We could lay on the floor for hours or across the bed, looking at this huge Tupac picture on his bedroom wall. He would smoke, and we would talk. He was a great friend who loved me to pieces, but due to circumstances, we could never be together.

However, during one deep conversation about relationships, he said, "Bee Bee, I wish I could see the world through your eyes!" Then he laughed and, looking at me, said, "You sincerely believe that everyone is good!"

"They're not!"

He was scolding me for not requiring people to earn my trust. By doing so, I'm inadvertently allowing myself to be hurt. He advised me to take control and demand that those around me earn my trust before I give it freely. This way, I can protect myself and ensure that only those who truly deserve my trust have access to it. He emphasized that this behavior is not cool!
"B.B.!" he screamed, "Wake up, they are very cruel! Don't give everything away for free; make people earn your trust. You have a beautiful and genuine soul, but not everyone is like you. You are like the kind lady at the gas station who talks to strangers, lends them a dollar, and they promise to return it when they go back to their car, but they never come back. You have already lost too many dollars this way. Stop giving everyone dollars. They're not coming back.

Be cautious about giving your heart to someone because I wasn't always in protect mode with mine. Don't give them an A-grade right away. Start with an F and let them work their way up to a good grade. Don't give your heart to people who don't deserve it. You are a valuable person and should be highly regarded by someone. If you keep undervaluing yourself, others will continue to take you for granted because you let them."

When I heard this, I froze like a deer in the headlights because I had been allowing people to exploit me. I didn't know how to regain my power, but the message was clear: STOP GIVING THEM A BOX OF MATCHES. It's like waking up to a fire you didn't even know was burning.

It's important to remember that in both personal and business matters, I always strive to be generous. However, being a generous person can sometimes make you vulnerable to those who take advantage of your kindness. It's important to be cautious and observant of the people around you. Some individuals who claim to be your friends may actually be pretending while secretly draining your energy and envying your good nature. It's not you they dislike, but rather your kind-heartedness.

People with good hearts often face criticism. It's crucial to stay away from people who engage in manipulative behavior and to be mindful of any warning signs. These individuals may be gathering information about you in order to imitate your actions and replicate your success. However, they pose no real threat to you or to the path that fate has set for you, as they are just one misstep away from their own downfall. Furthermore, it's comforting to remember that according to faith, your enemies will ultimately be humbled. Therefore, all you need to do is step away and keep your eyes open.

If you are starting a business, investing, or dressing for success, watch out because they may follow suit. If you speak eloquently and articulately, they may also change their speech. Therefore, keep your vision hidden from them because the Bible speaks of seed being stolen before it ever hits the ground. Watch your company so you don't wake up in a fire.
So, who is holding the match again?

### *What is your foundation built on?*

Life is about building a solid foundation. The solidity of your foundation depends on the "soil samples" of your life. If the soil is contaminated, what you build or attempt to build will be delayed, denied, or destroyed because of where and what you are building on. You can't build something good on something bad, and you certainly can't build something strong on something weak.

Just like any project, it starts with a blueprint, an outline, a vision, a passion, or simply an idea of what you want. You'll find that your original plan might be altered for many different reasons, but alteration or change is not always a bad thing. In fact, it's inevitable. If something goes 100% according to plan, I'd be worried. Look at it as an enhancement or a way to perfect plan A. You want to strive for perfection, but don't expect life to be that way. What do you learn if you live in a space where all things are intact? Our lives are shaped by many elements around us, but it's important to remember that we don't have to be defined by what we see, experience, or hear. If we find ourselves feeling unbalanced or broken at any point, we can always work on correcting our foundation.

Think of a building.

We often admire the impressive structures with their striking designs and intricate details. If I were to take you to a magnificent mansion right now and we stood in front of it, you might describe it as a stunning three-story, seven-bedroom, nine-bathroom brick mansion with oversized floor-to-ceiling bay windows. The home features several covered walkout balconies with custom French door access, some leading to the garden and others opening to an Olympic-sized saltwater pool. At the front, a wide, grand split staircase leads to massive glass double entry doors.

It's easy for us to focus on the surface beauty of the mansion, but there's always something missing in the description – the foundation! No one pays attention to the most crucial part. No one says, "Look at this fantastic mansion and its double-reinforced foundation, poured with blood, sweat, and tears." Why? Because it's out of sight, out of mind, and often overlooked. We don't see it. But isn't the foundation the most important part of a building?

It's only when a full inspection of the structure is carried out that most people start paying attention. Issues with the foundation could cause damage to the entire structure, leading to collapse or sinking. It could result in massive destruction if not corrected.

Now, I'm looking at my life and realizing that we have to pay attention to the foundation on which we're building everything. If I had to unroll the original blueprints of my life for you, you'd notice many changes marked up and scratched out in a variety of colors. Those colors are alterations that had to be made along the way of my build. The original plan won't stay the same, ever.

There are numerous versions of myself noted on those blueprints by volume or revision. You have to have the edits and versions of your life noted or documented to ensure you are operating on the most current plans for your life. If you do not pay close attention, you will find yourself operating again on version 17 when you were clearly on 38. Why? Because you revert to what was comfortable or familiar. You find yourself back in the same situations and relationships. This is not forward motion; it's backpedaling. Maybe it is fear or the fact that you took your eyes off the plan, the prize, your vision, and your future, and for the moment, it feels good until you see smoke.

My thoughts as it was happening to me were numbing. I allowed someone (or something) to insert themselves in a blueprint that didn't originally include them. That was an alteration. I was back at the drawing board, often revising previous plans to see if (A) fit into my current life's events or (B). Was that why I scratched (A) in the first place? You must know that one in the load-bearing walls of your world is about to fall. It's important to not allow that to fall or else the home will be destroyed.

Let's take a look at your own foundation. Ask yourself this question: What is my foundation built on? What do the soil samples look like? You will not know if you don't look at it. Step back from your life like an out-of-body experience and take a good look at YOU! How are you presented to the world? What DO THEY SEE?

---

Is your life centered around finances? With money being the driving force behind your job, side hustle, and relationships, does it control everything you do? What happens if that financial stability disappears? I see a potential disaster brewing because how far are you willing to go to maintain that financial security?

Perhaps it's not finances but relationships that form the core of your life. Maybe you're like a log cabin built on the foundation of relationships with no solid structure in place. Each wall represents different aspects of your relationships - friends, family, business dealings, religion, and money. Is this structure strong enough for you?

Maybe you're built around the image others have of you. It's an image you feel compelled to maintain, constantly seeking validation through social media likes, moments, and followers. You may appear fabulous on the outside to those around you, but the truth is that it's all a facade. When you strip away the material, the true pain is exposed.

We are like clay being molded by a potter. Each of us will look different when the potter's hands release us, and the wheel of life stops spinning. If we are not shaped well, we will collapse when the spinning stops because our foundation is weak. We cannot shape ourselves; most of us rely on the inner strength of our faith.

When we are not connected to it, our energy is not as positive, and our lives are influenced by experiences and toxic words and beliefs of the people we allow to influence us. The books we read, the things we watch on TV, and the internet all become a part of who we are. We need to be mindful of who and what we allow into our lives. Evaluating who we trust and what we allow in our space is important to ensure it adds value to our lives.

Let me show you what it would look like to be taken out of the hands of others, pulling the strings of our lives, and put in the hands of the Almighty. The large, wet hands are placed on a big piece of clay on a flat plate. Suddenly, the plate starts to spin slowly. The creator of this design begins to form the clay as it spins around and around. Because the hands stay moist, the clay stays in place in the hands of the creator. It goes from huge chunks of clay to a formation of something, but here is where things can go wrong. The wheel starts spinning a little faster when the creator starts shaping and thinning. The clay, still in mold form, starts getting weak and begins to slouch and lean until it wobbles and falls over. The creator looks at the suddenly lifeless clay and puts his hands back on it, starting to form it all over again. Not even to his surprise, the clay does the same exact thing. It begins to wobble and lean until it falls over. Now he sits, pondering what he could do to make the clay whole, stronger, more durable, and resistant to the spinning. It seems too fast for the clay, so he slows down the wheel and spins it slower. Then, he decides to make the clay a bit thicker.

Sometimes, we just need a little more support to help us through tough times. This support can come in the form of patience, love from genuine people, recognition for our hard work, daily hugs, positive affirmations, and signs that reassure us we're on the right path. These are the things that help strengthen us. Once we have this support, it's important to slow down and take the time to learn and grow instead of rushing through life.

We need to embrace our purpose and understand that we're meant to hold an extraordinary amount. Our goal is not to be reduced in size but to learn how to support the capacity of what we've been given.

As we continue with our journey, we'll face challenging situations that will test us like never before. These are the moments when we're being transformed and strengthened. This process will remove any impurities and unnecessary parts, leaving us sturdy and ready for whatever comes next. In the end, after all the challenges and growth, we'll emerge as a masterpiece.

Such is life! There will be many times when God must come and rescue you from yourself. Did you hear what I just said? Not from the claws of someone else, but from yourself! You are your very own enemy. In times of self-destruction, we must learn to allow the hands of the potter, who is God, to reshape us. There will be many more times in your life when you will slouch and stumble, but it's the hands of that gentle touch on broken places and the smoothing of rough places that move us through the process of purification, healing, and development to get the best design crafted just for you.

My 'pot' (life) is different from yours. Put me on the shelf next to you, and we might look identical to the naked eye as big pots crafted out of clay, but there are grooves and moves in my clay that existed solely because the soundtrack of my creation was orchestrated under different elements. It might have even taken my pot longer to be made because of the havoc and mayhem of my circumstances.

You are not alone, and your designer, the all-knowing God, had a plan when he picked up the clay of your life and called your name.

# Chapter 8

NO MORE BBB

(BACK-BURNER BEHAVIOR)

# ~8~
# NO MORE BBB
# (BACK-BURNER BEHAVIOR)

*Welcome! Here I'll take your crap, lies, disloyalty, abuse, rejection and deceit. You don't have to love me in return as long as you don't leave. I believe in you, and I know one day you'll believe in me as well. Enjoy your stay.*

That is what was written on the doormat at my heart's entry. It was because I wasn't seeing my value. When you are unaware of your value, you allow everyone just to do whatever they want. That's NOT OK.
Your days of being devalued end here! Even if that means going M.I.A to get reconnected to who God has called you to be. WE HAVE TO STOP MISSING THE MARK in our lives. The only reason you are missing it is because you have not set a metric for the standards of operation for your life.

A few years before I was remarried in 2015, I had become so fed up with pain. You know, being hurt, being left behind, feeling like I wasn't good enough. I decided there was only one way to protect myself: go into hiding. No, I didn't move to Utah or some state where I didn't know anyone; I hid myself in God.

Maybe you are unsure how to do this, but it is not complicated at all. Just surrender! My surrender looked like this.

One day, I sat down in all my tears and brokenness and screamed, "I CAN'T DO THIS WITHOUT YOU, LORD! Please! Don't leave me in this place!!!!"

It's okay to cry and break down. You can't go through life without experiencing tough moments. If you try to avoid them, you'll still feel broken. When your heart becomes hard and cold, it's a dark and broken place. It's one of the worst valleys to be in, as it makes it even harder for others to reach out to you. You may not even want to be reached. Sometimes, you may think that you're perfectly fine and everyone else around you are the ones with the issues.

When I cried out, it was because I didn't want to go to jail. I knew in my heart that the next person who crushed me would send me over the top. I said to God that I was going to go to prison for life if he did not hide me under his wing and protect my heart. I was over the pain. I couldn't breathe. I could not blame the people I was dealing with because that was my choice.

We all have a choice, yet we want to be loved so badly that we put up with so much. I was trying to be honest and transparent. I cried out to the Lord, asking him to help me. My exact words, after I regained a little bit of my composure, were, "Lord, please hide me so far under your wing that it would take a man who knows you or has a strong desire to know you to lift up your wing and say, 'Can I have her?'"

My desire was to be so hidden in him that he'd have to have God's permission to take me.

This was the first step in me protecting my peace and staying out of jail. I had to seek help from above! I was a mother to four lovely daughters and realized that I needed to love myself more and protect them from the possibility of losing their mother. I felt like I couldn't handle another heartbreak. Though I didn't have many relationships, by the time I turned 38, I had been through enough long-term and short-term situations to recognize a pattern of deceitful individuals.

The process of hiding myself away was about finding my connection to my faith and rediscovering my identity. It was about learning what I truly liked and disliked, what was true and what was false, what was genuine and what was fake, what was sweet and what was sour. I needed to learn that it was perfectly okay for me to say NO, stand by my decision, and truly mean it. I had to learn the sound of my own voice and not just the sound of my silence mixed with the thunderstorm of tears. My tears had their own voice, and it was a voice that sounded terrifying.

If you have ever experienced a severe thunderstorm that frightened you to the point of feeling paralyzed, then you have encountered my tears. As a little girl, I believe I stopped breathing, and I had to relearn how to breathe again. She felt trapped, and I realized that I needed to learn how to help her break free. I had to work on my own self-talk, learning how to affirm myself and have honest conversations with myself when I looked in the mirror. It was important for me to learn how to love and accept myself, acknowledging my beauty, intelligence, and achievements.

Unfortunately, many of us seek validation and approval from others, tying our self-worth to the people we are with or the situations we are in. When we don't receive that validation or love, we can lose ourselves. We end up believing the labels others put on us instead of embracing who we truly are according to our faith. I'd like you to reflect on where life has taken you and who has influenced your self-image. It's important to remember that our worth is not determined by the opinions of others but by the truth of who we are according to our faith.

Personally, I reached a breaking point where I felt like all the pain, I had experienced, was going to bubble over and overwhelm me. That's why I needed to take a step back and be hidden for a while. I needed God to help me alleviate the pressure that had built up in my life. During that time, I was able to grow stronger, happier, and healthier. I found a sense of peace that was truly invaluable. God showed me that I had an identity crisis; I had always been so focused on being everything to everyone else that I didn't really know who I was. With His guidance, I was able to discover how to love myself and embrace my true identity. In doing so, I became Beatrice the Boss.

She was a strong and resilient fighter who refused to accept no for an answer. In addition, I finally understood Buttafli. The writer! The poet! The songstress! She hid her pain in the secret places of her heart but exposed it in her art. She used any color possible to expel the pain via a rhyme, rhythm, verse, or bar openly on a mic overflowing with emotion and snatched the ear of the listener who re-lived the hidden places of her brokenness.

I got help from Bee Bee. She was the little girl trapped in a world she thought never wanted her. A world where she didn't feel as though she fit in and was challenged with not wanting to live because of the tormenting dreams of her abuse and the strain of wanting to feel like she belonged. Every day was a decision to try again, and that try again would either be to try to live or try to die.

Her fight to live was stronger than her fight to die because she found peace in writing where she could escape the world; she felt the world was unforgiving and unkind. I thank God for allowing me to meet myself at different phases of my life and heal forward. I was finally able to see that woman I had been daring to become.

Don't think that just because you hide yourself, there won't be moments of temptation to sneak out from under Daddy's watch. I snuck out a few times, and each time, I paid the price for my peace but not the price of losing my freedom because some of life's steam had been released, so mentally, I was in a different place. But that space brought an awareness to what was love and was not because now, I was looking at things from a different vantage point.

When we are not hidden, we do things that the flesh desires and not the desires of God for our lives. It makes you feel dirty, devalued, sad, and disappointed. You'd feel you violated your parents' trust. But God already knows the remorse of your heart. You don't have PERMISSION to continue to misuse the life God has given you.

I violated an agreement made to myself and to God. I violated the hard work and efforts to protect my peace. We must learn to let God Love us. His love covers and protects you from yourself when you surrender all of the places of your life. He wants to be a part of everything, not just the bad things but the good, the big, and the small. The mind and the heart cannot deceive you. Once you decide to protect your peace, don't fall back into your old ways and old thinking patterns.

The last time I strayed away from God's protection was in January 2014. I met a wonderful man named Zell, and as we got to know each other, we discovered that we had grown up in the same church and our moms sang together in the choir. We had even sat near each other in the children's choir on Sundays. Knowing this made it easy for us to connect as adults, and I found myself letting my guard down and straying from God's protection once again.

For a few months, we were completely captivated by one another. It felt as though our spirits were intertwined, creating an unbreakable bond. We were enveloped in a surreal world of mystical powers, fairy dust, and soft clouds, experiencing the most beautiful sense of calmness and peace. Our conversations were intellectually stimulating. Whenever we were together, it felt like we were floating in the air. I will never forget the first time we kissed. An unexplainable energy passed between us, and we both felt it without question. It connected us in a way that was impossible to ignore.

Our energy terrified me. He seemed like a dream come true, but I knew I wasn't the only one feeling this way about this guy. I thought, "No way, he was a one-woman man." So, I had to make a choice. Do I keep moving forward with this thing that feels amazing, knowing that the bottom will certainly fall out, as it always does for me? Or do I cut my losses early and protect the peace I had been working so hard to find? I decided to see what would happen because, even for the moment, it felt too good to let go of. Every conversation and time we got together took my breath away. After kicking it together for about three months, God showed me pieces of Zell.

During a Sunday service, Pastor Ken stepped up to deliver his message. I had pen and paper ready to take notes, but as he began to speak, I couldn't hear anything coming out of his mouth! It was like my ears were closed, but I could see his mouth moving. Suddenly, I heard a very audible voice and instantly knew it was God. It wasn't a conversation because I wasn't in a position to speak back to God. It was like I was in dictation mode, and I could still see Pastor Ken's mouth moving when I lifted my head, but not a word he spoke. I began to write down everything I heard the Lord say to me. It was crazy because he was talking about Zell.

After completing my writing, I ended up with four pages filled on both sides of a five-by-seven notepad. On the first page, he expressed how he had forfeited many things simply because he didn't know how to ask me for help. He requested my assistance, but what he plans to do with it will be his decision. "He will ask you to help him pray as he doesn't know how to connect with me. He may mention that he has lost his faith or is struggling to find it." God continued, "Ask him to be honest because there are still others in the background. Ask him if he's ready to give me a yes. I've been chasing him since he was a little boy. I was with him when the bullet went past his head. If he chooses you, I will take his business and life to another level. And YOU will search no more; YOU will never hurt the way you have previously."

I was blown away by how much was on the baby and felt so blessed that God would come and share with me. That was enough for me to know that this man was mine if he accepted that God had answered his request.

I was so confident in what God had said that when he asked me how the church was that day, I didn't hesitate to tell him that God had spoken to me about him. He was very intrigued by that and told me he wanted to know exactly what he said when he came over for dinner. Later that evening, after dinner, we were watching TV, and he said, "I want you to help me increase my faith." I smiled and said, "I know." Then he said, "I think I could have been further in my business, but I just don't know how to ask God about it." I said, "I know!" Finally, he said, "Maybe you can help me learn how to pray." I chuckled and said, "I KNOW!"

He sat up, looked at me, and said, "How do you know?"

I told him because God had already told me. I asked him to walk over to the bench and grab the paper from the jeans pocket. He did, and he brought it over to me. I unfolded it, and we began to read it. For me, it was as if I was reading it for the very first time. I couldn't even recognize my handwriting. It looked almost like hieroglyphics to me.

After we both read together all of the things that God had spoken to me that morning, I think he was a bit confused. He may have thought I was part of Dion's psychic world! No, I was no kin to the psychic Dion, lol. I just heard from God. But Zell had never disclosed to me the things God had spoken. There was no way I should have known some of the things on that paper. But I did.

Another fire was coming to the surface.

He stayed the night. And the following day, while he ate the breakfast I prepared, I did something STUPID. I slid him a key and said, whenever you are ready to be here, you can.

LORD, why did I do that? It was out of character for me to even have a man who was not my man in my home or anywhere near my kids. I did not bring random men into my private space. But he wasn't random, and now, because of what God had spoken, I was sure this was my new life.

How many of you know when God shows you a glimpse of something, you can move too fast outside of God's timing? I did just that. God did not tell me to pressure or invite this man into my world. Clearly, he said IF HE CHOOSES YOU!

We get so hung up in part of what we hear that we do not take time to allow God to be God. So here I go with a book of matches! Striking, lighting, and fanning a new fire.

Zell took the key from the table after breakfast, kissed me goodbye, and that was it. It was unlike us to not chat, text, or talk multiple times a day. However, that day marked a turning point as there was silence. After we stopped talking, everything became eerily quiet. However, within days, I started experiencing sharp chest pains. This was completely out of character, and I knew exactly what caused it. It was the key that I gave to that man. I realized I had pushed him too hard and expected too much from him too soon.

I was sharing things I had learned from God and then gave him a key, ultimately driving him away. I felt like I was living in a scene from the movie *Disappearing Acts*. It seemed as though the great Houdini himself had made everything vanish into thin air. However, now I felt like I was suffocating, choking on my tears at night. I felt abandoned and rejected, and that old familiar feeling of never being good enough had returned. My vase full of marbles had started to manifest again, and I couldn't help but wonder what I did wrong. I hadn't changed, yet someone once again deemed me unworthy.

It had been several weeks since I had experienced that amazing feeling, and I found myself struggling to get through each day. I cried, sobbed, and mourned the loss of it. My church held a marriage conference that allowed singles to participate. During the conference, I asked a question: How do you date as a single when all you know is how to be a wife?

I didn't know how to be a friend, a side piece, a girlfriend, or anything else; all I knew was how to be a wife. I would "wife" everyone I dated, which had only been a few guys since my divorce. I didn't understand any other role. God created me to be this woman, yet I was still alone.

I cried my eyes out during the entire marriage conference and had to leave early because I was not in a good place emotionally. All I wanted to do was hide and seek forgiveness from the Lord. Later, while sitting on the toilet, God spoke to me (I know, it sounds funny, but I often hear from him during my bathroom time). He said that the difficult situation I was going through was a temporary inconvenience that would bring permanent improvement. He also told me not to be discouraged by appearances; it was not rejection but protection and redirection. He then instructed me to delete all the pictures, messages, and contact information related to the situation. Before doing so, he told me to send one last message, which he specifically instructed me on what to say. Following his guidance, I sent the message and deleted everything related to the situation. A few weeks later, with my faith fully restored, I moved forward with my life.

I had a problem, since I had tested the waters of being in a relationship. My body and flesh are now craving the connection or company of someone. So, I prayed a lot and stayed locked away in my home. I starved those cravings with exercise and workouts at the gym. This allowed me to shift my focus and move forward.

We must be able to hear from God and be led by him. I know I continue to say it, but I must say it again… It's not the people around us who always inflict pain on us; it's us who inflict and allow things to happen based on the choices we make. I could have chosen differently and not even considered the possibility of being swept off my feet. However, I made a conscious decision, aware that there was potential for both positive and negative outcomes. We don't always enter such situations with our eyes closed. We notice the fire, but we believe we won't get burned.

When God speaks to us, it's not always a command to take immediate action. Sometimes, He just wants to show us a glimpse of our future and asks us to be patient. However, I didn't follow this advice.
Within eight months, I lost 50 pounds and gained clarity and peace. I felt whole and protected because of my strong connection with God who saved me again from my own destructive tendencies.
One beautiful November day, the sun was shining, and the weather felt almost like spring. I was wearing my favorite jeans and a white sweater, and my hair and makeup were on point. Feeling confident and happy, I started taking selfies.

As I stood in front of my favorite tree, I said to myself, "Girl, you look so fine!" That's when I heard God's voice say, "Send him a picture!" I laughed and responded, "You have quite a sense of humor, God." I wanted to send a picture, but I had already deleted his contact details from my phone. However, he insisted that I should send the picture and suggested that I say, "Happy Holidays!" along with it. I reminded him that I didn't have his phone number since he had instructed me to delete it. He then suggested that I send an instant message. Since I believe in obedience, I agreed and sent the picture. I didn't expect anything to happen, and I went about my day and weeks, eventually forgetting about the picture.

In late December of 2014, I had another wonderful day. It felt like a beautiful spring day, and this time I was wearing my cute boots, denim jeans, and a red sweatshirt, and once again my hair and makeup were on point. I was glowing once again! I was standing on the back deck, next to my favorite tree, when God spoke to me again. Our conversation was the same as before. He said, "Send him a picture, but this time, say Seasons Greetings, and I wish you a prosperous New Year!" Without hesitation, I obeyed and sent the picture. This time, I didn't even question God's instructions.

After I tried to put my phone in my back pocket, I received a notification sound from my messaging app. I was surprised that he had replied. We exchanged a few messages that completely had me captivated all over again. He apologized to me for vanishing and explained how his fear and life at the time didn't allow him to handle us appropriately. He also said the fear was my consistency which he was not accustomed to, He then said he'd love to take me to dinner but he knew my RULE would not allow that.

You're likely curious about "The Rule", how it works and why it is necessary in the first place. Let me explain.

I've always given my best in the first round of a relationship or marriage. Because I invest everything my heart can offer in round one, I don't believe in giving anyone a round two. Let me clarify what this means to me: it signifies that I have exhausted all possibilities in the relationship and provided that person with countless opportunities to make the right decisions and address any issues we faced. Once I have reached my limit or if the other person has chosen to end the relationship, I find peace in my pain and never look back.

I firmly believe that after all the hardships I've endured, if I were to give someone a round two, it would be out of a desire to completely destroy them and inflict the same pain they caused me. However, because I know that I am not meant to be that kind of person, my rule of "No Round Two" keeps me from experiencing jail time or regret. I have never gone back on my word or returned to a past relationship. For me, the first round is the only round.

Zell was neither my man nor my husband, and we never had a formal relationship. We simply spent time together without any title or commitments. Or as I told him, we were kicking it. This meant the rule to protect myself from getting hurt in a relationship didn't apply to him.

Our date was set for January 9, 2015, at Gulf Shores, a charming local restaurant. We faced a 30-minute wait to be seated, so we returned to his truck and enjoyed watching a movie together until we received the notification that our table was ready. It truly was the sweetest date ever.

From that moment on, we have been inseparable. He joined me at church a few Sundays after our reunion, and our connection deepened on a level I hadn't anticipated.

As the weeks went by, he surprised me with an unexpected declaration: he wanted to marry me. The proposal was anything but traditional, starting off with a simple question, "What are you doing Tuesday night around 6:00?" I replied confidently that I would be at Bible study with him. His response, "Great! The Pastor wants to meet with us" left me utterly bewildered. My mind raced with thoughts, and the first thing that came to me was panic—I didn't want to join the Praise Team; I was perfectly happy just sitting quietly in the pews.

Curiosity gnawed at me, prompting me to ask, "Why does the Pastor want to meet?" His answer took me completely off guard: "Oh, we are starting marriage counseling!" In that moment, everything clicked. It wasn't just a casual night at church; it was the beginning of a journey I had only dreamed about. My heart was racing at the thought of what was to come. Our bond was no longer just about companionship; it was about building a future together, grounded in faith and love.

I couldn't have been happier when he said that. Things were moving quickly, but he was determined not to let us ever be apart again. It was refreshing to see a man truly take the lead—something I wasn't accustomed to in my previous relationships. His decisiveness was both comforting and exhilarating. Less than a month after we began marriage counseling, we were married in a beautiful ceremony at the church on Wednesday, April 22, 2015.

The moment we tied the knot, an overwhelming sense of peace washed over me. I felt as though God was revealing something profound: had He brought him into my life at the start of our relationship, it could have led to my own downfall. It wasn't that he was a bad person; we were simply at different stages of our lives, both needing time to grow and heal. I realized that God was still working on us—cleaning us up for what lay ahead.

I believe God knew that even though my heart had been broken when he left, that "alone season" allowed me to rediscover myself and strengthen my faith. It taught me the value of patience and the importance of preparation for what was to come. With him by my side, I felt ready to embrace our future, confident that our journey was part of a greater plan.

This is why God prompted me to send that last text before I obediently deleted all previous traces of him. In a nutshell, my message conveyed, "I'll still be here."

It's crucial to recognize that disregarding commitments to oneself and God can have serious consequences—sometimes, everything can be at stake. I acted impulsively regarding something God was preparing me for, but thanks to His grace, the situation was eventually restored in my life.

I learned that I can no longer wrap my life up in a big box with wrapping paper and bows and hand it off to anyone. Putting my happiness first was no longer optional my husband made sure. With my husband's support, I learned to establish boundaries and stand my ground.

Before God sent my husband my way, I was delusional about love. I loved based on how I felt inside and what I believed others wanted and deserved. But my husband loved me from a different place in his heart, and honestly, it felt awkward—not because his love was awkward, but because I wasn't used to being loved that way.

He gave me random hugs, spontaneous kisses, and compliments the moment I opened my eyes in the morning, and sometimes even while they were closed, he would kiss my face. It was strange because no one had ever loved me that deeply or intimately. At night, as I lay in his arms, he'd squeeze me tightly and say, "This is the best part of my day!" What type of love is this? I'll tell you: it was a love I had to learn to embrace because it was so pure.

This is what love was and is—a feeling that makes me feel safe and cherished. From day one to the present, it has not changed. In fact, it has only grown stronger and extends to all the kids and grandchildren.

**Outside of God's Love for me, my husband's love is honestly the ONLY thing I'm ever sure of.**

After our grandson's passing in December 2023, I realized I had been living my life for others and their priorities. It was a wake-up call that inspired me to live life on my own terms and not put my happiness on hold anymore. Despite the difficult circumstances, I adopted a fighter's mentality and chose to focus on pursuing the things that bring me joy.

I thought I was loving and supporting my friends and family, but I realized they were using me. They took advantage of me, and although I considered them to be important people in my life, they never reciprocated my kindness. It's like the saying goes, 'If you see a sucker, bump his head,' and sadly, I was that sucker.

I didn't extend my hand to help because I wanted to be known as a savior. I did these things because I honestly believed it was the right thing to do, and I hoped that at some point in life, they would be able to do the same for me. Every year, I would push the things that mattered to me to the back burner, thinking I would return to them later. However, they would end up being put off for weeks, months, and even years. The most frustrating part is that some tasks never finish, no matter how long I put them off.

I was exhausted. Exhausted from fake, uncaring, unmotivated, inconsiderate people and situations. Life's fires are all about what we go through. Every chapter of our life's story is built brick by brick of intentional and unintentional events. We are looking for someone to blame while NEVER taking ownership or accountability for the role we played. I have stayed in some friendships and relationships for way too long.

Something deep down inside of me said that they needed me, and that was both true and false. They needed what I was willing to give them, but not me. I was like a human resource center for all things related to them, including finances. I'm not bragging about that. I'm crying over it because I allowed myself to be used. I never knew that I was being used by people who wouldn't even spit on me if I were on fire. These are the same people who would never bring a bag of groceries to my address or even pay for my lunch if we were eating alone or in a group.

Foolishness, just utter foolishness on my part.

The pot on the back of my stove is overflowing with all the things I've put on the back burner for the sake of others. Every time I add something else to it, the pot seems to grow and overflow even more. It's become a constant reminder of all the things I've sacrificed and delayed in my own life. It used to be just a small saucepan on the back burner, but now it feels like a never-ending campfire with an enormous pot. I'm tired of neglecting my own needs and desires and putting them in that pot. It's my own fault that my life is overflowing with delayed dreams and unfulfilled aspirations.

My grandson EJ used to tell me, "GMa, you need to take care of yourself too. Make time for things that make you happy." EJ taught me how to persevere and live my life, no matter what I am going through.

Today, take a page out of a 9-year-old's book when he says you need to take care of yourself, too! Decide that the value of your life is important enough to move you to the front and vow never to be pushed to that back burner again. It can be intimidating to finally step out in faith and pursue the things that make your heart sing. However, God didn't take the time to instill all those valuable tools in you just for you to bury them in the backyard. You may not know exactly where to start, but I assure you that this is the perfect place JUST START!

You have walked through many of the hottest fires of my life, and there are countless more that I haven't even shared. But guess what? I'm here right now in this moment with you, sharing how God kept my foot from slipping. I survived to tell you that you are next in line! I still come across a marble or two hidden in the corners of my world, but I no longer run and hide from those marbles. I face them head-on and keep moving forward because, more than anything, I deserve to see how the story ends. Despite all the struggles I have faced in life, I remain unbroken. I see myself as a daily work in progress, but the joy of truly understanding who I am and learning to navigate the challenges that make me powerful and resilient is an invaluable experience.

I will live this life full on purpose and die empty. Why? Because someone is waiting to experience my story. Someone has been waiting for me to speak up and share my feelings, as it gives them the strength to acknowledge the hidden joy they may have overlooked during their pain. Joy in pain? Yes. If you confront your pain instead of wallowing in it, you can find the joy of freedom that comes from showing the world that you survived. By doing so, you can also help someone else who is watching you navigate their own struggles.

For the fires or challenges in our lives to persist, three elements must be present: heat (which represents disagreement), fuel (which encompasses reminders, words, or actions), and oxygen (symbolizing unforgiveness and uncontrolled anger). Additionally, the chemical reaction consists of aggression, impulsivity, and a lack of boundaries. When controlling fires, we must avoid heat, fuel, and oxygen to prevent a chemical reaction from occurring.

Once you can identify, manage, and process the fires in your life, you can then focus on moving in a direction that helps you create the life you were meant to live. Prioritize the things that ignite your passions and align with your purpose, while also assisting others based on the boundaries you've set. Now extinguish the flames and heal. Use the soil as a place to rebuild the life you were destined to have.

*Healing Starts in the Middle*

## *God Whispers*

One morning, God asked why my book hadn't been published yet. I was defensive, saying that it was too late and that everyone was an author now, so why bother publishing it? God replied, "Because I told you to."

I remember when he told me that my books would produce healing from the inside and then manifest on the outside. He explained that although his people appeared to be doing well on the outside, they were all broken on the inside. He said my books would go inside and produce the healing needed to manifest on their exterior. He went on to mention that my books had a unique signature or design that set them apart from other authors.
When I asked him to elaborate, he said that chapter one started in the middle. I was confused, as it is not customary for a book to start in the middle. However, he explained that this was intentional, as it was symbolic of where healing starts - in the heart of man. So, he suggested that my readers open the book in the middle to start reading and then flip it back to the front to finish.

His words left me in awe, and I began to reorganize the table of contents accordingly.-----

He took me back to when I was 9 years old and bought my mom that birthday card *(You will read about this in chapter 6)*. At that time, I only saw the pain and missed the purpose; I felt the agony but did not feel the anointing. I thought her words were rough, but they really were love.

God showed me that buying the card and writing in it was the first time I indeed became a writer. It was my mother's response that encouraged me to start journaling, writing poetry, and expressing myself through ink and paper. She even gifted me a typewriter because she knew how much I loved writing. He showed me that I carried the heavy weight of her response with me like an anchor around my neck, and she never knew how that one momentary reaction changed me.

I did not realize that I had a calling to be a giver, to show genuine compassion and help others who may be silently suffering. The experience of the birthday card was a turning point that brought out the kindness and empathy that was already inside of me. It was a necessary moment that helped me become the person I was meant to be and not a fault I needed to blame Mom for.

It is crucial to keep in mind that each person has their own unique perspective, which means they may perceive things differently from one another. This is an integral part of your individual healing process, and every detail holds significance. I would like to encourage you to concentrate on your own narrative and avoid diminishing your pain solely to shield others in your story. If you wish to heal, you must be willing to confront the truth.

There are two types of pain: the one that causes you deep hurt and the kind that drains you and everything around it.

    I want to encourage you to trust God.

When you feel that He is calling you to do something, don't get discouraged by any delays. Some people may tell you that opportunities come only once in a lifetime, but that's not true. When God has a plan for you, He will bring it back to you. All you have to do is choose to obey Him. He will accomplish His plans with or without you, but it's always better to willingly follow His calling. Unfortunately, many people ignore His call until they go through a difficult experience. So, don't wait for that to happen. Choose to do what you are called to do and trust God.

At 48 years old, I was forced to sift through my ashes. It was then that I finally realized that my mother was the source of the spark that ignited a great gift within me. I learned that not all fires have to be destructive.

# Welcome to the fire!

*You are about to have an experience and the only way to truly understand what you're about to read is first to take a deep breath and allow this to play in your mind like a movie. It's easy to get caught up in the words of the stories, but I encourage you not to miss the message while I walk you through the scenes of the fire.*

Hi, thank you for joining me for the walkthrough of the aftermath of a few of life's fires. These fires had many random explosions. It's often difficult to pinpoint or even determine where a blast will occur when one doesn't know the source of what sparked the initial event.

As your guide, I will personally share with you what the evidence proved to be fact; we will be accompanied by someone who knows everything. There is a fourth man in this fire. Come with me and let me introduce you to God. He will be joining us for several reasons. He is joining us because he has an assembled team to help restore this devastation. Yes, He is an Engineer. I know him as the only one who has been able to assist me during and after the fires of life. He will keep us safe while navigating dangerous hotspots while revisiting the scenes.

He was able to find the black box, which is our surveillance system. It is something that is downloaded into each of us. You may know this also as YOUR MEMORY.

It captures everything from start to finish, even the things done in private that no one ever saw or knew about. Sometimes things are happening so quickly that you can't even remember all that is taking place. God takes note of everything and doesn't forget anything. He is armed with what you need to be put back together as well as explaining how you ended up in your condition.

Remember, as you walk through this life's playback with me, don't lose sight of God. He is the only one who can safely get us in and out of this. That's part of the promise to us when we enter with him. Come on, follow me as I follow him.

Be careful as you enter this room. Watch your step because there are a lot of broken places and falling objects in here. Watch your head! You almost bumped into abandonment.

As you enter this part of the home, you will notice the fire was more aggressive, and there was a chemical explosion on the other side of that wall. That wall had a lot hidden behind it, and no one saw the buildup until it was too late. The explosion caused damage to everyone within proximity to it. You will have to wear a mask in that area because the stench of pain still fills the air, and if you breathe in the heartbreak, it could cause irreversible damage to the lungs, your heart, and even your future.

 Now, you're about to enter the side walls of my mind. But let me warn you, my thoughts are all over the place, but I'm sure your brain does that to you as well. Thoughts are hanging from the ceiling like pieces of a broken ceiling fan. If you aren't careful you might get lost trying to figure out your way. There are several rooms in this house to walk through. So many fires to explain yet so many things to uncover in the ash. I pray you find personal healing as you journey through the rubble of my fires.

# Chapter 1

## OUTBURST OF MY SOUL

## *I'll fix your clothes, Momma*

The smell of onions, bell pepper, cooking grease, and beef fills the air. The sounds of the vinyl crackled over the words of her favorite holiday music. I can still see the pretty, big, red porcelain bowl sitting on the table. She seems so happy singing and moving her hips to the song *What Do the Lonely Do at Christmas*.

Then, I hear what sounds like bumping and stumbling, and suddenly, he appears in the kitchen doorway. I felt the energy being sucked out of the room as she stopped in her tracks and looked up. He moved sluggishly into the room where my sister and I were watching TV and listening to her sing. One by one, he sat us on top of the refrigerator as he has done so many times before.

THEN--------------
-------------IT STARTS------------

He hits her!!!! Over and over and over again. I can't hear anything outside her cries and stuff falling to the floor. I'm dying inside because things are hitting the floor, being thrown great distances, and getting flipped over.

We are helpless.

I see the bowl fall from the table, smashing into many pieces. The gravy in the cast iron skillet is starting to bubble but I can't even hear our cries. I don't even know what my sister's emotional state is because I'm lost in transition.

In my mind I can see and hear the ironing board when it falls over. I hear her cries. Her cries are piercing me like knives because I'm hurting for her but too little to help her.

It seems to have lasted a lifetime, even though the truth is the tornado-like movements were merely 10 or 20 minutes. Somehow, we were no longer on top of that big old refrigerator. But who in the (you know what) turned the stove off?

Was this maniac conscious or sober enough to turn it off himself because he didn't want it to burn? And then leave!!! Really? Really?!
I walked down the now, dark hallway, and followed the muffled cry, knowing she was in tears. The loud sounds of words repeatedly scratching on the record player, "What do they do, what do they do, what do they do at Christmas?" filled the dark hall.

Finally, I see her and the aftermath of the explosion, which had just swept through the rooms on Kensington Ave. She's sitting in a rocking chair, rocking back and forth with blood and tears combined. Her beautiful blouse and bra were ripped and hanging down the side of her body. I took a step closer, looked her in her face as I cried, and said, "I'LL FIX YOUR CLOTHES, MOMMA... I'LL FIX YOUR CLOTHES!"
This was my first fire. Unbeknownst to me this would be the first of many and it was going to take me a while to realize I needed to wake up and put the fires out.

I WAS FOUR YEARS OLD WHEN I WOKE UP IN MY FIRST FIRE!

# ~1~
## OUTBURST OF MY SOUL

It was as if someone had pushed me out of the bed! The sound of the alarm ringing loudly gave me notice that SOMETHING was not right. I immediately responded by running to see what, where, and why. What is causing the alert? Where is it coming from? Why is it giving notice for potential harm?

Something isn't right!
After several minutes of running around like a chicken with my head cut off, I can't seem to understand why this dang on ALARM is screaming. It took even longer to realize that the problem was not in my home; it was in my SPIRIT. Something in my life was on fire; there were alarms, sirens, bells, and the horrible sounds of screeching cries.

I am in trouble, and now I am standing outside watching everything that has ever meant anything to me disappear in a roaring blaze hidden in black smoke. How do you process anything when there is no escape from the inevitable?

At that moment, your lungs collapse as you reach and gasp for air to breathe. Your vision is blurred as the tears fill your eyes before they spill down the front of your face. Your mouth becomes dry because glands are suddenly blocked. Nothing comes out! No words, no sound. You can't scream, you can't shout, you can't grunt, because you are numb. Numb! You allowed a fire starter to enter your space and strike one match that destroyed everything you had inside.

In the fires of life, you don't always have time to stop and figure out where the smoke is coming from when everything seems to be burning down all at once. There are times you see the smoke starting, but you once again got distracted, too busy doing absolutely NOTHING. Then, as soon as you walk away from one small event that seems minor, you are running to put out another fire. See, these fires that have taken something from you have been known to come in many different forms. Maybe, just maybe, one of the following scenarios fits a fire you can relate to.

## *Fire 1 - The Abortion*

Were you the girl who had the abortion because he said it was the right thing to do? "We are not ready to have a baby yet," he whispers. You loved him so you honestly thought he was looking out for YOU as he leaned in saying, "I LOVE YOU." You know how that is when the person you love makes decisions about your life, but it only benefits them. They are quick to give you the "it's for the greater good" pep talk. So, you went along with it, but he was nowhere to be found after the event. Night after night, you wake startled, all alone, no HIM, no BABY, and in tears because you thought you heard the infant cry in your sleep. You feel like you are losing your mind. That's just the start of your story, but you lost something and WOKE UP IN THE FIRE. Your alarms are ringing.

### *Fire 2 - The Abuse*
Were you the innocent guy or girl who was sexually abused, and now you are having issues attempting healthy relationships because you just can't seem to trust anyone? Because the violation of your life happened so early, you fear getting close to anyone. Or maybe you are out there bad because fear is setting in, and you hide in meaningless relationships going from one to another because you're searching for that feeling of being loved, yet missing protection. You get involved with everyone that comes your way, batting an eye, telling you that you're sexy and you're what they need in their life. You engage in all sorts of compromising activities to learn later you are being used. You lived the role of being victimized, and they took full advantage of that imagery. What else did you expect? Whether you're male or female, you find yourself feeling empty with the never good enough mentality. You're stuck in that feeling, but you still give, give, and give because you somehow believe that maybe, one day, someone will see you. But they won't boo. I'm sorry to tell you, they won't see you because you don't see you. You attract into your life exactly what you see and think about yourself.

My God, someone just WOKE UP IN THE FIRE! Your alarms are ringing.

### *Fire 3 - The Lonely/Unloved Child*
Are you the woman or man who never saw momma or daddy love anything outside of work, money, sex, drugs, partying, friends, and those streets? It's ok. You don't have to be embarrassed to answer this question in your heart. You can't get free of what you won't address.

You never received hugs and kisses from the people who were supposed to teach you the most important thing in life: LOVE! You may have learned how to make money and get men or women to give you whatever you want, but wasn't that also at a cost? You use your body to feel connected to something or someone. Perhaps you used your intellect and smartness to assist someone in building themselves up. People used you to further their visions or get good college or high school grades. You became an architect of building up people and their businesses, their dreams and empires, but, ultimately, got left once they got what they needed. You never saw kindness, affection, attentiveness, loyalty, trust, or PURE untainted LOVE. So, you travel this journey of life without true purpose.

You have no idea what love looks, feels, smells, or tastes like. Trust me, it is not tasteless. Love is so sweet. But, because of your disconnect with love, you never understood how being in a relationship with GOD gives you access to experience love so purely. His essence is peaceful and calming. You never understood how something as simple as LOVING yourself would transform and transcend into a gift far more precious than material possessions. Do you not understand the real value of loving yourself? We all think we love ourselves, but when we look at how we allow others to handle us, and situations to impact our environments, we learn that we are not showing love to ourselves. You have an obligation to take care of YOU! This is the mental, physical, and emotional parts of you. We teach people how to honor and dishonor us.

Love can be sitting, standing, or even walking with you, and you are clueless. You miss what you can't recognize. You mistreat it, abuse it, talk nasty to it, abandon it, and ignore it simply because it was faceless to you. Love is like medication to a sick heart.

The body is smart, and it often tries to reject foreign substances. Think about some medications. Sometimes they don't work because the body says no, or they cause a reaction that makes you sick. It's like a two-edged sword. It can either protect or harm the receiver. The incorrect dose of medication or drugs can be fatal. This is why it comes with instructions. But love is sooo different. It's a good medication that you really could never get too much of, and even though it doesn't come with instructions, being loved properly will not kill you. The body naturally wants to reject what it's not familiar with.

I hate to compare love to illness, but let's look at this from the perspective of what it is. Not wanting or recognizing love or encountering it tends to leave people living unhappy lives. Some people die from a lack of love, loneliness, and grief. When someone has never encountered love before, they reject and fight it, and even sabotage the idea of it because it's a foreign feeling they can't explain.

How can one accept what they don't recognize? If a person knew love before, it's recognized immediately, and embraced, but if they didn't, the reaction is fear, uncertainty, rejection, and possibly even SHOCK. This is why people start acting out and pushing it away from their system. Can you think back to when you rejected love because you didn't realize then that it was just that? Now, all these years later, you look back and say WOW, that was real, and I could have experienced it?

I think someone just WOKE UP IN THE FIRE. Your alarms are ringing.

### *Fire 4 - The abusive relationship*
Are you the person who found yourself stuck in an abusive relationship that you desperately wanted to be free of? You were too afraid and embarrassed to tell your family or friends. So, day after day, you wake up in fear of living in a perfect storm. There is no escape, and all you want is out. Your existence is being poisoned with the toxic venom of this monster's bite.

Wait, maybe you are the abuser!
You don't want to be this person, and you are not even certain why there is so much anger inside you. You are even more confused as to why you are inflicting all the pain on the one person who seems to be with you, and you secretly cry because this savage demon of anger will not allow you peace. No matter who you are in this scenario, safety is compromised, and you are WAKING UP IN THE FIRE. Your alarms are ringing.

### *Fire 5 – Self sabotage*

Are you the guy who had a great girl on your side but didn't realize it at the time? You would call her your ride or die.

She would do anything for you. Right? If you required one breath to live a moment longer, she would unselfishly give it to you, not realizing or not even caring that it would end her existence just to give you one more minute on earth. Amazing!

You didn't see her, did you? I mean, *see her*. You never fully acknowledged who she was to you. You took her for granted. You took her kindness for weakness because again, you never saw her. Her desire was to make you smile as she maintained loyalty, honesty, dignity, dedication, and sincerity. Most importantly, she loved you without question more than she loved herself. But again, you were blind. She was beautiful, both internally and externally.

Your response to her love was full of selfish, sneaky, deceitful, disrespectful, and unloving behaviors. There was no loyalty, and you were unsupportive. The worst part is that you were this person to her on purpose. You honestly believed she would never be strong enough or courageous enough to strike back or finally leave. … then that day comes. That's all it takes for a person to wake up, and when they do, it could be silent or like waking up a sleeping tiger.

In the days of my father, they would say, "Caught you with your slip hanging" or "You got caught up."

Once that person wakes up, there is no need to assess the issue. It has gone too far; therefore, the only response is NO MORE and move on. You may be on the verge of losing the one thing that ever meant anything to you, but it was your choice. You are not bothered now because you believe she or he will not leave me! She needs me. She can't make it without me! I have this in the bag. But you don't, and here is where the reality check kicks in. She/he is NOT COMING BACK!

She found herself by digging deep within, and when she found herself, she discovered an inner strength that not only allowed her to leave but also fueled her future. Now, you begin to slowly feel as if you can't breathe and may even be coughing or choking as you gasp for air. Tears pouring down your face. I'd take a wild guess and say that's the smoke filling your lungs. Get to the floor and crawl fast to the door because YOU JUST WOKE UP IN THE FIRE. Your alarms are ringing.

There were several moments my alarms were ringing but it took me a while to finally wake up.

### *The Fire That Broke My Momma*

---

I was about 12 years old when our home caught fire. My grandparents bought the home in the early '50s after migrating from Mississippi for better opportunities. Most people would call our home a 2-story duplex, but in Saint Louis City, we call them two or four-family flats depending on the number of doors. We lived in the upstairs unit, and my grandparents lived downstairs in the first unit of the property. In the early '90s, my three cousins and aunt moved in with our grandparents for a short period as they transitioned. My other aunt, Willie, and her husband lived in the one-bedroom basement of the home.

It's crazy how, on the morning of the fire, my memory recorded a certain peace and utter chaos. It was a beautiful summer day, very early in the morning. I'd say about 9ish. Out of one eye, I could see my pretty, soft, buttercup yellow curtains flying away from the window because of that sweet, strong morning wind entering. I rolled back over on my face and sank deep into the pillow.

My little sister kept coming into my room saying, "BeeBee, would you make me some panycakes?" That was her way of communicating when she wanted to act like the baby, which she was. She was maybe 10 years old at the time. Usually, I would get up and do it, but I was genuinely enjoying sleeping in.

It could not have been 20 minutes later when I heard the loud, aggravating sound of the fire detector beeping out of control. We were used to this stupid thing going off daily for no apparent reason. It was as if someone walked past breathing and triggered it. Crazy right? My stepdad would constantly change the batteries, but at some point, we just believed the darn thing was possessed. Man, my mom would get that broom and beat it until the thing flew off the wall and the battery were hanging on for dear life. Most times, we would ignore it, and it would stop. But this wasn't one of those days.

My body popped up so fast from the comfort of the sheets and pillow, and my feet were on the floor. I'm not sure why I had this feeling, but I ran right over and slid the door open. (Follow me, and don't get confused; I had to slide the door open because we had this folding accordion-style door that had a magnet that would catch on the wall and secure it until you pulled it away from the magnet.) I looked to the left towards the kitchen at the alarm hanging on the hall wall. Then, quickly to the right, where the open/loft TV room was at the end of the hall. My heart immediately sank to the floor. All I saw was flames shooting through the room.

The flames were all over the back of the sofa and out the window. The sound of them seemed to roar and buzz and crackle louder than anything I had ever heard. As I ran toward the step, I screamed to my stepfather, "THE HOUSE IS ON FIRE!" The room that was on fire sat directly over the last four or five steps, therefore, I was running straight to the fire to escape it. Have you ever had to run to the danger to escape it?

I ran down the 17 stairs, out the front door, and onto the front porch. I began to hysterically beat on my Granny's door, which was directly to the right of our door. She came to the door as I was beating and screaming, "Fire!!! FIRE!!!" Very calmly, she said, "B-A-B-E, what are you saying? Me and JC just came in from da store. Ain't no fire child." Now, what you must understand is that my grandma is from Yazoo, Mississippi, and she had a very strong country accent. "Grandma," I screamed, "The house is on fire!" So, as the family started hearing the breaking and cracking of glass from above, they believed me.

I was standing outside in a pair of panties and a tank top with all my 12 year old boy-like body exposed. My cousin ran out and gave me some shorts. My grandma kept trying to run in the home saying she had to grab the deed to the house. In her era, paperwork was very important to them as there was no electronic copy she could pull up. So, getting the deed comforted her in knowing she could prove ownership. They would never believe their ownership existed without the documents they kept safely put away.

Reflecting, I don't even know if my sister was with me. I don't remember when she or my stepfather came out of the home. I remembered seeing her outside sometime later. It was said that my stepfather had tried to put the fire out with a few cups of water, but that fire was way too large for cups of water. We also later learned the room had been painted with oil-based paint, so the water was more of an accelerant.

I ran to the neighbors to call my mom at work to break the news to her that her home was on fire. I said, "Mom, you have to come home. The roof is on Fire!" Years later, we were able to laugh about it. She said she thought it was a joke and was even singing at work, "The roof is on fire, the roof is on fire, the roof is on fire!!!! We don't need no water; let the (blank) burn..." Okay, you get my point if you know the song of the era.

Once Mom arrived, she saw everything she had worked hard for destroyed by what looked like a five-alarm FIRE. In reality, it was considered a three-alarm because they had to call in a total of three different fire dispatch districts to support extinguishing the blaze, which was extremely intense.
The American Red Cross, all the local television news networks, and The Saint Louis News journalists were on the scene. Nothing could have ever prepared me for the emotional breakdown I saw my mom have.

Reporters snapped pictures of her during this traumatic WTF moment. She could not stand to her feet alone; her legs just gave out as she nearly fainted several times while her screams of "Oh My God, that's all we have in the world" filled the air and roared even louder than the flames. The sounds of her cries and moans seemed to overtake those watching as many attempted to comfort her. All I heard and saw was Momma. I saw the pain she felt and, in that moment, I died inside because I could not help my mom or save everything, she had worked so hard for. That was so hard for me to see- her broken. She'd never voluntarily had vulnerable moments in front of us. I saw her as many things but never broken.

I used to prepare for important mental and life-changing events like this because we used to have fire drills and conversations about what we would grab, how fast we would grab it, and how quickly we would escape. But when that demon of flames entered our lives that morning, all I could do was RUN. Nothing about this fire went the way I thought it would. The fear was so real and not something planning would prepare us for.

That was a real-life fire. It came with real smoke, real fear, and real firefighters, but all the FIRES will not present themselves with flames or smoke, and there won't be a group of firefighters ready to dowse the flames and get you to safety. Newsflash! No one is coming to save us from life. If by chance we are lucky or blessed enough to have someone walking through these fires with us, we must remember they are a support, not your savior. **<u>THEY CAN'T SAVE YOU</u>**! That's a you and God thing! Your support is only there to hold you up when you begin to fall because that is inevitable.

# Chapter 2

FIVE ALARM BLAZE

## *Are we Good?*

I saw you today, right at the intersection of uncertain and 100%.
I was confused as to why you would be in that space.
You have always been a master of maps and direction, so to see you sitting in there, disconnected, troubled me.

I replayed the previous days and months in my head in hopes of unveiling a motive for your disorientation, yet I found none.

We--- aren't 100% anymore?
How did I miss this?
There used to be a time when there was no doubt about who we were... to each other and with each other.
Now you've turned away, leaving me on All This Love Circle, and you're drifting down.
I thought I saw something better interstate.
Why did you say yes?
I would've respected it - I'm not ready yet.

**(Spoken Word Written in 2005)**

## ~2~
## FIVE ALARM BLAZE

**You've got to go through the fire, before you can have the healing!**

For years, I allowed someone else's opinions to influence my decisions, whether it was terminating a pregnancy, ending friendships, mishandling money, and, most importantly, abandoning myself, my faith, and my belief system. I lived with the pain of those fires. My choices became my personal hell, and I was trapped in my mind.

### *The blaze was hotter than expected:*

When I was 20 years old, I was in a relationship with a childhood friend. The relationship felt easy because we grew up together, and I was best friends with his female cousins. He and his best friend lived together and often seemed inseparable. They were always up to something, both good and bad. They collaborated with their brilliant minds and started multiple successful business ventures driven by their passion for barbering.

I enjoyed spending time with him and eagerly awaited a chance to hang out. However, there were instances where our time seemed to clash with my mom's lengthy to-do list, which had nothing to do with me whatsoever.

Due to my decision for my one-year-old daughter and I to live with my mother, I often felt as though I had to be careful with my actions to maintain a peaceful environment until I could find my own place. Since I worked frequently and spent my free time with friends, I wasn't present at home very often. However, I'm not sure what changed, but my mother and I began to have frequent conflicts once I entered the relationship.

One evening, my mother asked me to wash and fold clothes belonging to her and my stepfather. I wasn't in the mood, and we argued. I had just finished a 12-hour work shift and was looking forward to some relaxation time with my friend Ronnie, who was already waiting for me outside in her car as per our plans. It was not unusual for me to do laundry since I had been helping my mother with their laundry since I was young. If I remember correctly, I started doing the laundry when my mom had multiple surgeries and could not go up and down stairs. However, the problem was that I continued to be stuck with it even after she recovered and throughout my adulthood.

Since my friend was waiting outside, I went to the car to explain my delay and dilemma to her while mom and I were having a disagreement. My mother warned me that if I left the house without completing the task she asked me to do, she would lock the door and not allow me back inside. I was feeling frustrated, but I didn't take my mother's threat seriously. So, I stepped out into the cold to let my friend know I would meet her later because my mother was being difficult. However, my mother was not bluffing when she said that if I left, I would not be allowed back in the house.

I went back to the door in the freezing winter temperatures, but I couldn't get back in. I had to plead with my little sister to bring me my coat, and even that was a struggle. Eventually, she managed to bring it to me. I got into the car with my best friend, tears streaming down my face, and we drove away. I was exhausted and used her phone to call my boyfriend. He simply said to come over and stay with him. I did just that.

A month later, he rented a U-Haul and moved my belongings from mom's house. However, I couldn't stay with him and his best friend due to their living situation. His friend was dating a close friend of mine but was not faithful, which conflicted with my beliefs. Being a guest in their home would have required me to keep their secret even though I was uncomfortable with other girls there. My boyfriend, being okay with his friends' questionable activities, made me think about the phrase, *birds of a feather flock together.* So, I decided to get my own apartment. Since I wasn't 21, he put his name on the lease with me.

Having a place was crucial for both my daughter and me. It provided us with a sense of independence, privacy, and security - things that are essential for a comfortable and happy life. I was happy that we were able to achieve that goal, and it had a positive impact on both our lives.

Things were going great for both of us. I was doing well in the insurance industry, and his business was becoming a popular barber's location in North County. However, every time things seemed perfect, something would come along to shake things up a bit.

In mid-April of '95, I realized that I had missed my period. While my partner wasn't particularly concerned and believed it could be due to work stress, I knew my body well enough to worry. Being genetically predisposed to fertility, I was anxious about what could be going on.

Receiving the news of a pregnancy couldn't have happened at a worse time. My partner and I were busy building a life together, and we both already had daughters to take care of. Now, I was carrying a little someone inside me. His reaction was not as calm as I had hoped when I told him about the confirmed news. Instead, it was clear that he was not ready to deal with this news at all. He reminded me that business was booming, and it wasn't a good time to plan any distractions. I was puzzled because this was not planned. Neither of us was thinking clearly when we were intimately exploring each other.

I was hoping he didn't use the one WORD that I hated. That ONE word some men who want to avoid responsibility slip in as though it's the start of a full sentence. I was bracing for impact because I also was TOTALLY against the idea of using it as a form of birth control. But, he said it!!! He said it with such assurance that it would be the right decision for the woman he loved; HE SAID IT. They throw it around so freely; yes, we fall in line because we think it will save our relationships. It doesn't.

He said, "Call that clinic on North Euclid. We have to go get this taken care of right away. You are still very early, so it won't cost me that much, but baby, THIS IS FOR THE BEST RIGHT NOW."

Despite loving him, I didn't agree that it was the right decision for us as a couple, a team, or a family. Even though I had scheduled the appointment, I still felt terrible about the idea of going through with it. I tried to convince myself that at the last minute, I would speak up and say, "YOU NEVER asked ME what I WANTED. YOU NEVER ASKED ME HOW I FELT ABOUT ANY OF THIS!" Between wanting him to think I was still TEAM US; I silenced the crying girl inside of me every time he came around.

The day of the procedure arrived, and I had spent the entire night on my hands and knees in front of the dishwasher with my face pressed against the kitchen floor, crying out to God. I begged God to give me strength not to go when he arrived. I was shattered, crying, "Lord, I can't go. I'm not going to go. I'm not going to go! I will speak out and say no, this isn't right, and though it will be hard, I will be okay." I didn't want to experience it. My eyes were almost swollen shut when he knocked on the door at 6:30 am. He walked in, leaned down because of his towering height, and embraced me. He said, "Baby, it's okay," as he wiped away my tears.

I took a deep breath in his arms and said, "Okay." Then, I grabbed my keys and walked out the door. He locked the door behind us, and we headed to the appointment in his car. Throughout the ride, I felt empty and ashamed, apologizing to God in my heart. We pulled up to the location, and protestors were all over the premises. I was terrified! He handed me a money order and said, "Call me when you're done." He was serious!

The sad thing about the situation was that it probably wasn't the first time he had done that. He seemed too comfortable with the dynamics of the situation. I got out of the car with my head held low due to embarrassment while he drove away. My heart was broken, and my soul felt like it left my body. I was about to go through an ABORTION alone and ashamed.

The procedure was the worst! I lay on a table in a cold room with ears full of water from my tears and my heart beating faster than I could breathe. They started the process, and my mind began to analyze the sounds I heard and the feelings my body was encountering. The sound that filled the room was like a hand mixer used to beat a cake. Why am I so stupid, God? Why did I allow myself to be in this position? Hey, did I agree to go through this?

When it was over, I sat numb in a recovery room. I called and texted him, but there was no response. I waited in the waiting room for about an hour after the recovery room, hoping for a message from him. Finally, he sent a message saying he was sending someone to pick me up. How insensitive!

Since my friend was dating his friend, he recruited her to pick me up. I was bleeding profusely. When she arrived, she had to grab a towel from her trunk for me to sit on as I was ruining my clothes. She got me home, got me in the bed, and sat with me. He never came. He popped up a few days after the procedure as if everything was normal. For me, it was far from normal. I would wake up at night because I thought I was hearing a baby cry. I was emotional, scared, and alone.

My daughter was such a blessing because even though she had no clue of my pain, she kept hugging me, wiping my tears, and saying, "It's okay, mommy."

A little over a month had passed, and I was still bleeding nonstop from the procedure. One late night, I said Lord, I know you're real, and I repent for what I have done, but I cannot live in this condition. Please, Lord, heal my body! I vowed that if he healed me, I would never under any circumstance ever do that again. Almost instantly, I stopped bleeding. Again, God was showing himself real in the fires of my life.

Can you imagine waking up in the middle of the night from the sounds of a hand mixer screaming in your ear? It was a reminder of that sound from that traumatic day. Yeah, that sound will never go away for me; it's permanently imprinted on my soul. I pray you never understand or experience termination of a pregnancy. It's a fire that water can't even touch.

While I was recovering from a moment of carelessness, I made a promise to God that if He healed me, I would never take that road again, no matter the circumstance. I am from a family of dreamers. I have learned to pay close attention to them. During this time, I found myself having more dreams than normal. Real dreams that you wake from your sleep in tears and must ask for guidance because God shows you things.

It was June, and I dreamed of a pitch-black night. I was standing outside and noticed that everywhere I looked was complete utter darkness. No stars were in the sky, and light could not be found. To the left of me, **FIRE!** To the right of me, **FIRE**! In front of me, **FIRE**! There were only tall red and orange flames, and I could feel the heat.

I stood there fearful and confused, and the fire kept getting closer and closer to me. It felt so personal. This fire was coming for me, and I knew it would overtake me at the rate it was moving. The straight-line fire was coming in all directions except behind me. So, I turned and started sprinting in the opposite direction. As I was running, the fire was closing in on me, and as it got closer and closer, it got hotter and hotter. Then, I heard a voice say, "If you let go, you can go faster." I was already running frantically for my life. Well, I didn't know what let go meant. As I ran, I looked all around, from side to side, up and down, and in my hands. I didn't have anything I could let go of, so I had no idea what I was supposed to let go of; therefore, with no time to spare, I decided to keep running. I was already feeling the exhaustion of running but decided that I could not or would not stop running. This fire would have to catch me and whatever I was holding on to.

Remember the baby from earlier? Did that small smoldering fire become a massive blaze that is now showing up in my dreams?

When I made the decision to keep running, suddenly it started to rain all over me. Rain was drenching me more than the darkness of the sky on me. There I stood in the pouring rain, facing these flames. I glanced around briefly, and I was standing in front of a storefront building. I'd never seen this building before but the fire could no longer reach me because the water covered me.

I know this doesn't make sense to you. It didn't even make sense to me then. But I woke up from that dream asking the Lord to give me a revelation.

My first thought was that maybe it was the devil. He was telling me if I let go of my boyfriend, I could go faster, but I quickly brushed that off, saying no, I wasn't letting him go. We hit a rough patch when the decision was made for me that we would delay the extension of the family so he could grow his barber shop and vision for his business. Although we were going through a difficult time, we were not in a place that required us to end the relationship.

In actuality, the dream had nothing to do with our relationship. God later showed me the voice I heard was that of the enemy telling me if I let go, I could go faster. It wasn't about a man, but about a promise I had made. The dream happened in June and was about to become a fore shadow of what was coming. I had to decide how I would respond to it early. When I decided to keep running, that set up protection around me for October.

That rain, well, it was God's way of saying I GOT YOU COVERED! That enemy, the FIRE, could not get to me with his protection. I had kept my word, not even knowing what was approaching. Going faster would mean reneging on my promise to God and although I had to endure hell, I stood on my word and God stood on his.

What was I thinking???

A few weeks after celebrating my 21st birthday, I found out I was pregnant with my son. I named my baby boy Emmanuel, but he lived only 10 hours and five minutes after birth. I didn't know he was a boy until the doctors informed me on the day he was born that he wouldn't survive. It was also on that same day that I was told I might not survive either. I remember thinking, who tells someone that? To understand this better, let's backtrack a few months before I learned the gender of my child.

When I was admitted to the hospital, I was three months pregnant. I ended up staying there for three months, connected to a morphine pump and a dermal tank, receiving heavy doses of pain relief around the clock. I was experiencing what I believed to be the worst pain of my life.

Prior to my hospitalization, I had been very sick and felt almost like I had the flu. I had become extremely weak and could barely get off the sofa. At that time, I already had a two-year-old daughter named TyAnna, who was smarter than any child I had ever met.

I had made several trips to the emergency room because I knew something was wrong, but each time I was sent home. I remember telling the doctors how sick I felt and expressing my concern that I might be leaking or urinating on myself, but they insisted I was fine. By that time, I had been sent home for the third time. Things became foggy after that, as what I remembered versus what actually happened would shock you. I recall taking a bath, and when I got out, I placed my left foot on the floor and stepped out. I saw blood gushing onto the floor, and the next thing I remember is waking up a few days later in a hospital bed.

I later learned from my friend and neighbor Keisha (RIP) that my baby girl found me on the bathroom floor in a puddle of blood. She went next door to the apartment in our building, knocked on Keisha's door, and told her that "Mommy was on the floor." My two-year-old saved my life.

Waking up in that hospital was just one of many challenges I was facing in my life at that time. I was no longer with the father of my son because I chose not to terminate the pregnancy he strongly encouraged. I had previously taken that route at his urging, but I made a vow to God that I would never allow myself to go through that again. We had been down that road before, and terminating the pregnancy was not up for discussion. I do not advocate for the termination of pregnancy, but as a young woman on my own, I had allowed someone else to make decisions about my life, and I went along with it.

This was the dream. This was the promise I made to God as a personal declaration, and no matter what cards life dealt me, I had decided to keep running forward. The outcome of this pregnancy would not ever be abortion. I was navigating through life-or-death medical issues, which certainly could end in a not-so-favorable outcome for me and impact my daughter. My life was making some crazy cyclone motion of wrong decisions because, while all of this was happening, I made yet another not-well-thought-out decision. I introduced a new small fire into the blueprint of my life: a future husband. You read it correctly. I was being wooed by the devil from the hospital bed.

I didn't think anything would come of it. The relationship seemed harmless, and he was a window of calmness in a time of chaos. Or so it seemed. Night after night, day after day, I laid in the hospital believing I was surely going to die, so having this interaction made me feel alive and gave me a little extra fight in my spirit. I never thought or imagined that he would become my husband. He was consoling me over the phone while I was fighting for my life in the hospital. I thought he was being a good friend.

EVERYDAY we talked, we laughed, I cried, he listened. He wasn't a stranger because we basically grew up together. How crazy is it that I knew him but didn't truly KNOW him?
Those late-night calls and early-morning check-ins meant the world to me. I was on my deathbed, and he would call long distances using calling cards to chat and keep my spirits up. He'd give me calling card numbers and codes so I could access him. (Many people reading this may have no idea long-distance calls used to cost big money and were paid by the minute).

One evening on a call, he said, "When you get out of that hospital, I want you to move to Houston. I'll take care of you." Something inside of me needed to believe that because (a) they had already told me I was going to die, and so was my child, and (b) it felt good to know that I could believe in having a different outcome. I started to consider I would NOT die. I also sold all my possessions in my apartment from the hospital bed. What I didn't sell, I had it stored at a friend's house temporarily. The only things I kept were my clothing and what my daughter Ty needed or would be looking for.

After I agreed to relocate, he began planning and encouraged me to survive the next unbearable few months.

How many of you know that you could be entertaining the antagonist without a clue? I had zero desire to shack up if God saved me from what I was going through in that hospital. I saw it as a second chance to live and possibly be loved. He had to marry me, which is exactly what happened, but I had an encounter before it all went down.

During this hospital stay, I rarely slept, and I was lying in the hospital bed full of doubt and lifeless at 3 or 4 AM. I did what many of us would do during this time; I grabbed something to read, and my go-to was always my Bible. Have you ever grabbed your Bible with the expectation that when you open it, it will fall right to a place that speaks to your situation and provides some guidance/direction? That was what I needed at that moment. I had been through so much, and the fires just kept coming.

So, I began reading Ezekiel 16, titled God's love for Jerusalem. Jerusalem didn't sound like it would give me any peace, therefore, I was confused about why I kept reading. I thought I should be in Psalms looking for messages of peace or comfort. Well, as I began to read, the story caught my attention. Why? Because of my interpretation of what I was reading. I am not asking you to have the same revelation but to follow along with me to understand how it shifted my future thoughts of who I am and/or who I could become if I weren't careful in how I navigated life.

As I read the passage that starts by talking about a baby girl, I pictured this baby born from two people who should not have been together. She had been ABANDONED!!! Thrown in the field alone, covered in blood and afterbirth. No one cut the cord, wrapped her in beautiful garments, or celebrated her entry into the world. God saw her lying there choking on her own blood because they didn't clear her passageway to breathe. No one had compassion; they threw her away.

I began to cry as if someone had just said my momma had passed.

It was 4 AM and I was balling out of control because I saw ME as I read the words! Not that I wasn't loved as a baby, and no one threw me away, but my heart was broken in the text because I, too, was abandoned in life.

Then the story goes on to say that God had mercy on her, and as He passed through, He saw her (ME) and said LIVE. WOW! The word LIVE was so vigorous to me. It was speaking directly to my circumstance.

Have you ever felt like you were dying because of the fire you were standing in? Have you felt like your fire of life would take you out? You knew it was going to kill you because it kept getting hotter and hotter or harder and harder? Have you ever cried so hard you could not breathe and felt like you were choking on your air and tears? Yes, me too, kind of like this baby choking on her blood.

But then God came by, saw you, saved you, and spoke life into your heart.

Now, in the story, not only did He call her to live, but He made her thrive and made a covenant with her. She began to grow up and blossom. She became more beautiful, and as she formed, her breasts became full, and her hair grew, but she was still naked, so the Lord took her in His wings and covered her nakedness.
He washed and clothed her in the finest embroidered garments and silk and anointed her with fine oil. He draped her in jewels around her neck and wrist, even put earrings in her ears, and placed a crown on her head. But when it said she even had a jewel in her nose, I knew he was talking about me. My finger touched my nose! My eyes got so large, like, OH MY!

Her table was full of fine flour, grains, oils, and honey because she had FAVOR with God. Her beauty was the talk. She was royal again because of God's splendor.

Now, here is where the shift happened.

She took that beauty and used it to play the role of the HARLOT. I had to sit upright in my bed like, WHAT? Wait, God, I'm confused! Now, suppose you have never heard the term HARLOT. In that case, it's the same as a sex worker, call girl, or prostitute, also known as a woman who has many casual sexual encounters or relationships and is most likely to receive payment of some form for her services.

It explained that not only did she act in harlotry, but she also poured out these acts to everyone who passed by. She took all the things our God had blessed her with, and she used them as an abomination by laying them out for her sinful acts and feeding those she entertained with the provision God had given her. She took her expensive gold and silver and melted them down to create male images she would use in her sexual sins. She built shrines and made high places for herself on every street.

She would have sex with everyone who passed through, but here is what got me. She was said to be worse than all the other harlots because she would not even accept payment for her acts of multiple harlotry. These men were to pay for services. Instead, she paid them! My mouth was on the floor, thinking, you paid them to come to you. No one solicited you. He said she was the opposite of other women who are harlots. He called her an adulterous wife who takes strange men instead of her husband. At this point GOD became incredibly angry because she was purposely provoking Him; He stretched out His hand against her and said, "How degenerate is your HEART?"

Things got deeper. God was so angry, and He said, this is what I'm going to do. Since you are so filthy and not thankful for the things I've given you, the covenant we had, the children and husband I blessed you with, I am going to call all your lovers and your enemies into one place, and I'm going to strip you naked in front of them. They are going to judge you like an adulterous wife or a woman who is bleeding. At the end they were going to burn down her home and kick down all the shrines. She would be stoned, and swords would also be fair game. This was a time of judgment that was being put down on her.

After reading this, I was terrified!

This was enough for me to call and wake my mom at 4 AM in the morning crying, saying GOD called me a HOE! To know my mom is to love her because she is crazy funny. Ethel said, "GIRL! Are you crazy? LOL, it is 4 AM! God did not call you no HOE!", while laughing.

I told her what I had read and how I thought God was speaking to me. But my mom reminded me that I was not doing the things the harlot did, so pray for understanding.

So, I did, and I read the chapter repeatedly, and God allowed me to see what He was saying to me at that moment. He showed me that I was feeling rejected and abandoned. Yes, I was choking on my life's disappointments and pains. Yes, I was feeling naked and exposed.

Yes, people had walked away and left, but God told me, "I have not left you. I picked you up out of that place and wrapped you in the security of my wings. I whispered in your ears every day that you are beautiful. I put the finest things around you and provided all the things you will need so you don't have to rely on the love of others because I LOVE you. I made a covenant with you and promised to protect and provide for you. I made you strong.

"But be careful, be very careful not to take the beauty of those things in your newly found strength and forget who I am and what I have done for you. It is so easy for you to get deceived by men or women who will make you believe they can love you more than I can. If you fall for it, you'll continue to seek them and their love vs me and mine. You will share with them what I have given you and your household. You will idolize getting love from people and things that will fail you. Do not go out seeking them, seeking their love and false affections as you will pay for it with your life."

My soul screamed because I was guilty of making decisions without consulting God. I am guilty of finding peace sometimes in people and not in him. But is that truly peace or just a piece of hell?

So now, as I lay in the hospital, I was mentally reflecting on what I had read and how there was some alignment with my own life. Remember when my baby found me in that pool of blood? Well, it turns out I had what was called an abruption; my placenta pulled away from the uterus. I didn't think I would ever get out of there. I made all these plans for my second chance at living without checking the temperature of those decisions with God. I was still very full of unresolved anger from previous hurt and relationships. I was in no position to connect with another before healing my wounds. Getting into a new unhealthy relationship that led to marriage was just another setup for a setback. It was me making more decisions again without consulting God.

While I was in the hospital, a good friend of mine was watching my daughter, and my mom would also have her. Often, that friend would bring TyAnna up to visit with me. I had become very exhausted and even uncertain about my life, and I wanted to check out. I was weary, depressed, and ready to give up. I had not eaten food in three months because of all the medication, and because of the pain, I was not able to keep anything down. So, it was IVs and liquids for me. When I entered the hospital, I weighed 145 pounds, and on the day that I was released, I weighed 95 pounds. I had not even paid attention to my smaller-than-normal frame because I was alive. I was walking out of one of the hottest fires of my life as a survivor.

I was supposed to die, and so was the child inside of me. But God had another plan. We don't always know or even agree with God's plan, but I trusted that He had a higher purpose and wanted me to be around for my daughter. There was a time or two when I would lay in bed just wondering what I had done wrong to deserve all the turmoil and torture I'd already encountered so early in life.

A song continued to drop in my spirit. I learned it from a friend of mine who had come to clean my house while I was sick prior to even being in the hospital. The song was called, *Just a Prayer Away*, by Yolanda Adams.

Day after day, I'd lay in that hospital bed crying and singing, "For I am just a prayer away, call my name with your heart, and I'll hear every word you happen to say, and when you cry at night, I'll wipe the tears away." That song got me through some rough days and even rougher nights. The other thing that got me through was seeing my daughter TyAnna.

My world was on fire, and I didn't know if I would see her after the fire. Seeing her gave me hope that I was strong enough to hold on. I knew the hospital said I wouldn't survive, but I also remembered my Grandma B saying, "My God is able to do ANYTHING," so I held on to that. My daughter gave me a WHY. She was so small, but she'd always rub my face and remind me (out of her mouth) it would be ok. One time, she even said I was going to be okay, but her brother was going to the sky to be with the LORD. She didn't know I was having a boy because at that time, neither did I. Everyone in the room cried when she said it, including the nurses. The emotion just overtook us all.

For months we had been trying to get my health insurance to transfer me to another hospital that was more equipped with a better neonatal ward and one that specialized in high-risk pregnancies, but it was such a challenge. During that time, I was on Medicaid, and the plan I was connected to was only linked to the Christian hospitals. How horrific is it to be laid up in a Christian or Catholic hospital where people get to make decisions for the lives of others with no regard for their wishes. You're sitting right there, fully capable of making your own decision, but your voice is silenced based on insurability.

One instance of this happened when the hospital arranged a meeting with me and other department heads, known as the Board of Ethics Committee. The committee was a combination of doctors, labor and delivery nurses, and hospital officials. The purpose of the meeting was to discuss and determine whether they were going to deliver the baby that had now been inside of me for several months without fluids. That's right, you heard me correctly. The baby had no fluids in the womb because my water had broken three months earlier.

When I was admitted into the hospital, they explained keeping me on fluids and comfortable in the bed was protocol for my condition, and there was still a possibility the waters could replenish. I was a little past five and a half months with a child sitting in my womb, and the daily pain was excruciating, even on Morphine and Demerol with basically no water/amniotic fluids.

This hospital believed I had lived an entire life, so their job was to fight to save the baby by putting me on bed rest and hoping the water would replenish or be enough to get me further along. The reality was they were waiting for me to either set up an infection or fever before they would escalate or see my case as life-threatening. Only then would they plan to remove the child from the womb. Well, because of the God that I serve, He protected me from both fever and infection. Medical professionals were baffled as to why I hadn't set up a fever or infection after all these months. Even in the physical state I was in, I still knew that there was a God.

The most heartbreaking moment was sitting in front of this Ethics Committee when the head nurse of labor and delivery said if they chose to allow early delivery of this baby and induce my labor, it would be considered abortion. She and her staff chose to work at a Catholic hospital, so they did not have to abort babies. Therefore, she and her staff would not care for me.

My poor little heart just broke. I was sitting there fragile, weak, and malnourished, hooked up to a Morphine and Demerol tank, still feeling pain, and she just told me that they were not going to fight to save my life. She was treating me as though I had some incurable disease, they were terrified to handle. I was being handled in that meeting as if I should have been quarantined or sent away.

After the meeting, they wheeled me back to my room. I cried my little heart out once they tucked me back underneath the sheets. There was a nurse named Elaine. I'll never forget her eyes. I truly believe she was an Angel who worked in the labor and delivery ward. She came in, and she said to me, "I'll take care of you." I cried, knowing there was at least one who had not abandoned me.

It was evident that I would not make it back home, and my son would not survive this. They finally told me the gender; it was a boy, confirmation of what my daughter had told me maybe weeks earlier, so I surely knew that God must have whispered it to her at only two years old. He sent me a message of hope.

I asked another nurse by the name of Brenda, who's certainly long gone and in her grave by now, if she would wheel me down to the hospital chapel so I could pray. She looked at me, chuckled, and said you can pray in your bed as she walked out of the room and closed the door. I was boiling over with anger, and I managed to get my frail body out of that bed, and I pushed all the chairs in the room up against the door. I told them not to allow her back into my room because that was a spirit I did not need around me.

What was I supposed to be learning from this fire? Would you agree that seeing the lessons is hard when you're in the flames?

Nevertheless, in comparison to what was to come, this was just a small smoldering fire. There was a blazing inferno brewing because I survived the trauma of childbirth. My premature son passed away after living 10 hours and five minutes. When I was released from the hospital, my Freddy Kruger nightmare was taking shape in the form of marriage to the man that spent three months, night and day, on the phone with me while I was in the hospital. This marriage though was camouflaged in love and affection. I was never prepared for the agony I had signed up for.

##  The Guilt of Trusting Others

WOW, even after that experience, I still didn't get how covered I was! I continued taking my life for granted and attaching myself to things and people who pulled me away from God and what I believed my life was meant for. I was like a giant magnet pulling more and more of the wrong people to me. Connecting and disconnecting from people who were bad for my energy, world, and life's journey. I was sharing all my innermost thoughts and visions with leeches who could care less about me. I was being played like a pawn on a chess board and losing massively. Truth be told, my life might as well be another publication of their favorite gossip platform or reality show because I promise every word would be repeated via the TiVo of life.

We must stop looking for friends to save us! As a matter of fact, let's STOP calling everyone friend! WHILE YOU ARE AT IT, stop calling everyone Sis or Bro!

I wasted so much energy and valuable years on people who were only wolves in sheep's clothing. God literally had to chin-check me! He said, "Stop talking to the mountain, talk to valley people! You share because you care. They don't. They sit at your table because they know they will be fed and can walk away with the to-go plate. They take more than needed because they're greedy, and you're too kind to stop them from doing it. You're trusting the wrong people and missing the signs God puts on your path. Think about how many times you've had the opportunity to walk away from those people, whether it was family or friends, but didn't or, shall I say, couldn't. Every reason or excuse in the book to be of assistance or pour into someone else, even when the relationship serves you absolutely no purpose. The funny thing is you don't really realize how devalued you are in the relationship or friendship until it no longer exists."

I noticed that when the friendships or our relationship was over, I didn't miss them even after many years. It was very clear to my soul that those people added no value to my life ever. They were just there sucking the life out of me. I didn't realize that life was being sucked out of me until they were gone, and I began to feel life again. Has that ever happened to you? When they are no longer in your life, suddenly you can breathe. It's like taking a handful of Altoids, chewing them real fast, and swallowing them, and now suddenly, your nose, throat, chest, and everything is open, and now you can breathe! That's also known as Peace of Mind. Or simply peace.

When this all sinks in, you watch it all go up in smoke. Brace yourself because the realization of the self-inflicted pain of those affiliations will overtake you emotionally. We wake up in these fires because we refuse to admit the obvious. We take too long to detach from the familiar. We treat the truth as if it is the boogeyman hiding in the closet, waiting for us to fall asleep so he can jump out and scare the living hell out of us. It doesn't have to be a dreaded experience. The fact is, you've already encountered the hardest part of dealing with the situation. It was inevitable. It makes no sense to continually allow small flares flying from your fire to coast past you. You must reach up and grab that ember!!

Now!! Right NOW! When you see it, knock it out of the air and make sure to put it out early. If not, you do nothing to prevent it from sparking an even larger blaze. Addressing the truth opens you up to transparency so the camouflage you have been using can be thrown away. You're acknowledging it is trash and no longer needed. You're afraid and hiding behind the mask. But. in the beauty of the truth lies power and strength. It will later be your story to tell and heal others.

I once had this conversation with God, and he told me everyone looks amazing on the surface, but inside, we are all on fire. We are screaming, and no one sees it because we cover it all with all life's material and superficial camo. He said when you see happy, it's simply dressed up and hiding behind war paint. People want to be happy but can't find an exit from the pain. They have lived there so long it starts to define them. Staying in that place is a choice. Either you want to be free or not.

I've searched through the many fires of my existence. I learned I was guilty of setting myself on fire a few times. Darn, maybe more times than I can count.

### So tired of the deception:

It's interesting how we often blame others for deceiving us when, in fact, the deception was our own doing. We chose to ignore or justify the signs and accept the person for who we wanted them to be.
When I was 38, I met this Rico Suave. With a proven track record in his profession and a mastery of the art of card playing, he was a true expert at navigating people and situations like a card game. He skillfully used his wit to turn the situation to his advantage. After discovering his secrets, I realized that I was just one of many women he managed skillfully. I admit he had the skills to juggle them all with ease. Once I saw the situation for what it was, I backed away because it wasn't a real relationship.

The situationship began at a time when I had started to find myself and realign my life. I was intrigued by his conversation and the idea of us enjoying many of the same things. He was charming and persuasive but spending time with him left me feeling gitty , yet drained, and my spirit was unfulfilled.

When we're faced with sweet talking, calm demeanor, intimacy, and gentle words, it's easy to deceive ourselves and lose focus. I thought, finally, things were going to be a little different. This is where we should start THINKING!

Now, expecting a different result by doing the same thing is insanity. Obstacles and tribulations are inevitable when you refocus your life's intentions. After much contemplation, I came to the realization that what I was doing was not in line with God's purpose for me. This insight led me to make the difficult decision to pivot my direction and pursue a path that is more in line with my calling.

I worked hard to revise my plan, but entertaining his ideas disrupted it.

In life, we all face distractions that can derail our plans. At such times, we need to refocus and realign our inner vision with our goals. Nobody with a clear and executable plan wants to deviate from it. If you have deviated from the path, returning to the correct course is simple. It's important to note that there is a significant distinction between being slightly off course and completely losing direction.

Honestly, I put myself in an uncomfortable mental space because it had more to do with someone paying attention to me. I had hidden myself out of fear of another self-inflicted knife in the heart.

I find myself repeating the same mistake, falling for the same trick. I had confidently laid the foundation of my new world, and the cement was almost dry when I allowed trouble to enter and walk around the construction site of my mind. It didn't make any sense! I willingly sabotaged myself, which is exactly what we tend to do.

I strode confidently, assured, and ready to face any challenge, certain I had rebuilt my mental fortitude on an unshakable foundation.

Through introspection, I have realized that my trusting nature has led to numerous heartaches in my relationships. If you have ever felt the same, let me tell you that it is never too late to make a change. With the right mindset and tools, we can learn from our past experiences and build stronger relationships in the future. Let me help you achieve that.

I have been through many painful experiences where my trust was shattered, leaving me feeling broken. It was time for me to take a step back and reevaluate how I approach trust in my relationships going forward. All in all, the impact may have been identical, but it's astounding how each took a different part of me. It's a testament to the fact that even the smallest differences in approach can yield drastically different outcomes.

Keep an eye out for small embers floating in the air. "Occasionally, I looked up and saw an ember right in front of me. It would then gradually burn out and descend slowly towards the ground."

Picture this: a bright flame shooting up into the sky, flickering and dancing as it rises higher and higher. But what goes up must come down. As the ember reaches its peak, it begins to burn out, gradually descending towards the ground in a slow and controlled manner. It's a beautiful sight to behold - the perfect balance of power and grace.

I will not continue to rebuild when my heart is set on something that will undoubtedly destroy me. It's time for me to take control of the situation and put an end to this madness. I refuse to let my desires cloud my judgment any longer. It's time to move on and start fresh. It's crucial to recognize the importance of identifying danger. After all, danger is danger, and we need to be aware of it when it's present. Unfortunately, we purposely ignore the sirens ringing. That's why we need to be vigilant in recognizing potential threats. By doing so, we can take the necessary precautions to ensure our safety.

Do we ignore what we hear, or do we not distinguish the sound of a siren from a doorbell? No one is coming to rescue me. No one is at the door! The door... that's my life! That's the alarm of my life screeching once again. All of us have ignored that warning.

Sometimes, when the tornado siren goes off while we are at home, we tend to casually look up, check the weather, and often do nothing about it because we've heard the noise before, and nothing has happened. Ignoring warnings can have disastrous consequences. It's time we start taking them seriously and make sure we're prepared to handle any potential risks. Let's not wait until it's too late to act.

Despite being able to identify fire hotspots, I made an error in judgment by testing the flames. It was a grave mistake, one that could have easily been avoided had I exercised caution and restraint. Let this be a lesson to all of us to prioritize safety above all else, even in situations where we feel confident and in control.

"Stay focused, avoid distractions, and don't deceive yourself."

# Chapter 3

EMBERS OF THE TRUTH

### I'm Empty

"How can something as simple as a plain piece of paper
Reveal the complexity of me?
There's so much clutter inside, yet I am still empty.
I am like a sheet of paper with 25 blank lines or so…
empty, blank.
I often wish I were half full, or at least I'd be
something other than empty.
The purpose of the paper is to meet ink, paint, pencil,
or maybe crayon, as the purpose of a heart is to give
and receive love.
For I am empty…….. 25 blank lines, empty."

**(Spoken Words 2007)**

## ~3~
## EMBERS OF THE TRUTH

Why is it so hard to face your truth?

You want everybody to believe you've got it all together. But the truth is YOU DON'T! Your perception of the truth is distorted. It's like holding a beautiful apple in your hand. From the outside, it's shiny and thick without bruising, and it even feels firm. But when you take a knife and cut that apple open, it's rotten at the core.

I'm saying that you're decomposing. There is a stench; even if no one else smells it, YOU DO. This is because you're dying on the inside. You show up all put together on the exterior, but if I could walk up to you and unzip the actor or actress in you, we would expose your interior.

The hurt, broken, agonizing, isolated, angry, depressed, injured, cut up, ripped apart, real YOU!

The you that's smashed down so deep in the pit of your belly that you literally feel sick in your spirit.

That version of YOU is crying out to be free from the suppression of decades of emotional pain. If you do not face the versions of you inside of you, YOU will die. Alarms have been ringing for so long that soon it will not be an internal siren; it will be an external one showing up and out in your actions.

Now is the time to declare I WON'T SELF DESTRUCT!

Your past traumas must be addressed if you want to live free. There is healing in the fires around you.

People are always telling me to change the story! You don't have to change the story. You must be willing to face the story. We can't allow the wrong people outside of us to convince us how to handle our eternal battles. Many are not even qualified to speak on how someone should deal with their healing. If we do not deal with the traumas of life, we will find ourselves trapped and tortured in the skin we live in. We cannot let unqualified voices from the outside dictate how we tackle our internal struggles. Many simply lack the knowledge to guide others in their healing journeys. If we ignore the traumas we've experienced, we'll remain trapped and tormented in our skin. Since I can't shed my skin for a fresh start, I must bravely identify and confront the fires that life presents to me. I can't take my skin off and get a new me so I must identify & address my fires of life.

I see people every day, and everything about them is fake. When you've been through things in life, you can look at others and understand where they are in theirs. We've all been there hiding in camouflage and putting nice flowers and paint around us to make the picture look prettier than it is. But strip all of that off, and you'll find broken, disappointed, rejected, hurting, lonely, unloved, abandoned, and mentally checked out. Do you know who those people become? They become abusers. They become great manipulators and chameleons.

I remember embers of my truth from a previous relationship with which I had no business entertaining.

He was married, and I was the woman I vowed never to be! I had no real answer as to how I ended up there, and sadly, I had no emotion toward the fact that I knew better. But my truth was, no matter how many days he spent with me, no matter how many calls and *I missed you baby* text messages he sent me, I was still and always would be THE OTHER WOMAN!!!!!

That's the real TRUTH! I had a book of matches, and I was sticking and lighting fires at will. It's self-inflicted pain.

Have you ever done something that made you sick to your stomach, but you enjoyed it in the moment? Yes, with my hand raised high. That comes from a place of brokenness. For me it was not just a place of brokenness, it was a place of disappointment and momentary acceptance. I was disappointed with myself because I knew God had not called me to be this person, yet my actions said otherwise.

Truly, there was nothing for me to gain except temporary relief from the pain of being alone. If you have ever found yourself here, I know you can understand. So, what was my truth? I needed help assessing it. What was the reason for my behavior? I needed to dig into this and figure out the source.

How in the hell did I become so absent-minded and careless that I was willing to accept someone who could NEVER love me at the capacity I needed, wanted, and so badly desired!?

Wait, wait, wait! I think I found an ember in my fire. I wanted and desired love so deeply that when someone paid 2.5 seconds worth of attention to me, I accepted it as a temporary fix to my deep yearning to be connected to what I thought could possibly fill the void.

What I realized is that the void gets bigger and bigger and bigger. It's like being in the sun for days without water, and you desire to quench your thirst so badly that even when you get a little taste of the water, it doesn't satisfy or fulfill the need; especially if someone only had one water bottle to quench your dehydrated state. That bottle helps for only a moment, but your mind and body will continue to crave it until it is satisfied.

People see relationships as a fix, but they are not the water that will rehydrate our souls and spirits! The Lord is the only true and living water resource.

This was a nearly catastrophic move on my part because I found myself kicking into reverse and no longer moving full steam ahead. I felt marbles falling out of my jar, and I wanted and needed to blame him for me becoming startled and spilling all the marbles.

Let's explain this jar.

You are walking around your life with this beautiful vase or jar, and every time there's an issue, a fire, a situation, a disappointment, or whatever it is, instead of dealing with it, you drop that marble in the jar. Each of these marbles has a name that speaks to the situations, traumas, events, or circumstances engraved on it. Now, the problem with this jar is that, at some point, it's at its capacity. Where else are you going to hide all these secrets and feelings? You're too afraid someone will see your dysfunction, so you keep it very, very close to you like an accessory. You find yourself in this place of new secrets and issues, then one day you wake up, become startled, spilling your marbles on the floor.

Pay attention to the marbles because you'll have to deal with them. They become lies in your hidden places because you hide them, not willing to face them, and they present themselves as deception. You can't just keep putting them in a jar; there's nowhere else for them to go, they won't fit, and they're falling out. This forces you to address the truths and your lies.

I realized this was one of those embers I had to take full ownership of! In these situations, either one of two things happens: either you knew he wasn't single from the start, or you found out sometime later.

I fought with the idea of entertaining someone who doesn't belong to me. I concluded that it is what it is. It's always going to end up very messy. You end up caught in your feelings and angry because he/she can't stay the night. You get so caught up that you hate when they get up and leave. Here's the tragedy. You lit the match that started the fire. You are now attempting to extinguish it.

It was an ember long ago, and now it's a full blaze.

---

### *I'm always fighting to be the me I see at a glance:*

In my mind, I often catch glimpses of a girl who is gentle and quiet, yet unabashedly assertive. She speaks softly and is slow to react. Despite her delicate nature, she is remarkably resilient. Her beauty is not solely based on her outward appearance, but stems from her inner confidence, charm, and devotion to her truth, as well as her ability to love in the face of adversity. She has no limits when it comes to what she can accomplish. She is fireproof.

I genuinely want to get to know her better. I want to talk to her and discover what she is really like. Did I mention that she has a smile that lights up the darkest evenings? Her eyes are magnetic and alluring. She is willing to bare her soul on camera simply because she is no longer afraid of who she is.

It took me 38 years to realize that the girl I was so eager to know was really me all along.

I was in love with myself. I was afraid of becoming her. She represented the part of me that I chose to love secretly, without allowing others to dictate her happiness. She was the healed part of me the version of myself before the pain and the one who emerged after I learned how to address and confront my own inner critic.

Healing is a process that has no endpoint. Therefore, we should always be in a state of repair.

How often do we claim to love ourselves because we keep ourselves well-groomed or treat ourselves to nice things? We sometimes think we love ourselves when we care for our health and wellness or eat nutritious foods. While these practices are all excellent ways to care for ourselves, what about the mental aspect of self-love?

Do you ever catch yourself using negative names for yourself or being overly critical of decisions that didn't go as planned? After experiencing a devastating event, what is your mindset? What thoughts go through your mind when you find yourself in a toxic situation or relationship?

Have you ever taken a moment to appreciate being free from anything that drains your positive energy? It truly feels as if you can tackle any challenge the world throws your way.

When you genuinely love yourself—I'm talking about real, deep self-love—everything changes. You will no longer allow people, situations, or circumstances to control you. They simply cannot have that power over you because you choose to take it back. Loving yourself is like telling the world, "Sorry, I couldn't hear your 'no!'" This means you refuse to be a victim of rejection or the chaos life may present.

You are ready to disconnect from that tumultuous world and tap into your internal power source. That power source is called ME!
ME represents the determination to keep your actions from leading you into a dark place.

ME is the understanding that even if something fails, I can pray my way through it and still be fine without negativity.

ME is like the emergency box on the wall that says, "IN CASE OF EMERGENCY, BREAK GLASS." That is ME!

Have you ever encountered a different side of yourself? Have you ever wanted to have a conversation with that part of you? Yes, I'm talking about you speaking to yourself! It may sound a bit silly, but if the positive aspects of you could step outside for just a moment to offer guidance or direction, you would likely find yourself in fewer difficult situations. Have you ever contemplated what you would be like if certain influences had never affected you or reached your core?

I've been pondering this for years. As I grow older, I feel I'm getting closer to becoming the person I admire within. I catch glimpses of her and wonder when I will finally become that person.

A persistent question echoes within me: could I have been someone different? What if I had taken a different path in my life? How many children might I have had if I had made a left turn instead of a right? While I cherish my children, I wonder how my narrative would have unfolded differently had I made other choices.

Imagine if there was a pivotal moment when I could have redirected my life. Would my destination have changed? Would my outcomes have been different? It's vital to reflect on this. Could it have spiraled any worse? We often perceive what we wish to see and cling to beliefs that comfort us, but there's no puppet master pulling the strings. We each have a hand in crafting our own journey.

Have you ever woken up feeling like you've been battling for your very existence? I have. One night, I awoke enveloped in a profound grief that had nothing to do with physical pain; it resided deep in my heart. Who wakes up in tears, questioning everything? I do! I felt immense sadness and loneliness, and I told myself, "Bea, you are truly a good person. You've sown countless good seeds, yet where is the bounty you deserve? Why am I waking up to stained pillowcases?" I yearned for my own fairy tale! Was it so wrong to seek more? I dedicated my life to loving and helping those around me, even those I was never meant to be connected with.

I felt like the universe, or God, owed me something. Have you ever been hurt because God didn't give you what you thought you deserved, when you thought you should have it? I often felt offended because I considered myself a good person who did good things for others. Yet, instead of experiencing happiness, I walked around feeling miserable inside while putting on a smile every day.

One night, with a pillow pressed tightly against my face, I screamed for dear life. My children were sleeping in rooms very close to mine, so I took special care not to let them see me in such a state. I wanted everything that God had for me, and most importantly, I felt I deserved it.

God had to remind me that He had already given me so much. Often, the more He gives, the more we want. We tend to seek financial or material blessings, but we often overlook the countless times He has been there for us. For example, how many times has He woken you up? Saved you from a car accident? Given you an extension on a bill just in time? Saved your child's life? These moments showed me how ungrateful my heart had been. To whom much is given, much is required. How could He bless me with even more when I wasn't a good steward of what I already had?

God walked me back through some moments of my life where there was no denying His presence.

He took me back to a very significant time in my life when I saw and knew I was not alone. I lived in Seattle, Washington, hundreds of miles from Saint Louis and my family. It was about 2 AM on my 22nd birthday, and I woke up with my (then) husband's hands wrapped tightly around my neck. I had been in a deep sleep and woke up suddenly gasping for air. He was sitting on my upper body with all his weight bearing on my chest, and his hands gripped firmly around my neck. As he squeezed my neck, he shook me ridiculously hard up and down onto the mattress. I was fighting and scratching and grabbing at his hands to get them from around my neck. Even though the room was dark, my eyes felt completely out of the socket, big and bright for cries of help. I could feel the tears rolling down the side of my face and into my ears.

That husband of mine kept saying you will make this hard on yourself. You are going to make this hard on yourself! I was so confused. I was confused because I was asleep, and I did not know what I would make hard on myself. I had not done anything. At certain moments, I could feel myself slipping away. It was like I was going in and out of consciousness, trying to fight. I felt like it was going to be the end, and I needed to have one last talk with God. In my heart, I said, "Lord, I love you, and I know you are real. If it is my time, then I am ready to go, but if it is not my time, I need you to get this man off me!"

It was as though a large man, whom I will always attest to being an Angel, threw my six-foot-three husband across the room and off my chest. It was like he was pushed off me with a great shove. He flew to his left but to my right and hit the wall. I hopped up swiftly from the bed, grabbing at my throat and trying to catch my breath while I was screaming thank you, Jesus, thank you, Jesus, thank you, Jesus! I'm most certain an Angel was in that room with me. I had no one else in Seattle outside of my daughter and my husband, but I had prayer, God, and some Angels watching over me. This, I am certain of.

There was another time when God revealed Himself to me in a profound way. He wanted me to understand that He had always been by my side, keeping and protecting me throughout my childhood. I believe I was born with an innate belief that people are inherently good. Because of this, I only saw the good in others and did not recognize the presence of bad people, which made me an easy target for those with ill intentions.

When I was about six years old, I remember we often had to get rides from friends because my mom didn't drive. She was a single mom doing what looked like, to a kid, superhero things. She was always a super mom to me, even when I was angry at her. During this time of her life, she worked in a local laundry, and I was in my 1$^{st}$ year of school or kindergarten. I got in trouble every single day. LOL. It wasn't because I was a bad kid but because I was super smart and loved talking. My teacher, Ms. G., used to whip my butt every day for distracting others. In the early 80s, teachers were allowed to spank kids because school was an extension of home. At least when I was growing up, it was allowed. My teacher had this yardstick called "The White Shadow." Dang, I got a lick every day.

It was not abnormal to get three butt whippings a day. Not only would the teachers get your butt, but the neighbors would as well. This was a real community. Everyone knew everyone, and families trusted each other. It was the village that helped raise us and keep us in line. If you lived at home with your parents and grandparents, you could possibly get spanked three times for the same situation. Once, it was by the neighbor who caught you doing something wrong. Then she called your grandma, so you got it from her when you got home. Then again, when your momma found out.

Not everyone is a trusting person, even if we were brought up to believe that all adults were right and almost like extensions of our family.

My mom's boyfriend wasn't a good guy, although she didn't realize it. Honestly, to this day, I still don't know if she was aware that he was an old, predatory jerk. She had a thing for older men. Am I wrong to think he might have been a sugar daddy? You know, someone who helps make ends meet, pays a few bills, or buys groceries now and then?

His name was Mr. Lawrence—a real creep! I know he's dead now because he was about 100 years old when I was 6. Since my mom didn't drive and got off work after school had let out, she trusted Mr. Lawrence to pick me up and stay with me until she got home. He would pick me up in one of those long cars they had back in the day. You know, the early 80s model 4-door spaceship looks like it would take up two parking spots in today's time. At first, I didn't mind going to his house after school. He lived down the street from us and had three levels on the very top level. It was like a game room with a pool table and other things. He was just trying to make me feel comfortable at his house. But then his comfort level turned into touching and showing himself to me. I was a little kid and didn't know what it meant or why he would even do it or want me to see it. But he always told me that we were playing a game and that with this game, it was a big secret and that we could not tell anyone. He asked me if I understood what secrets were. He told me that I could not tell my mom or anyone because then I wouldn't be able to play any games anymore, and I would get a whooping because I'd been a bad girl.

I didn't understand why I would get a whooping and be considered a bad girl. I didn't like the game because it made me feel very uncomfortable and unsafe. He would tell me to stop crying and be a big girl. I wanted to tell my mom or my cousin, but I didn't want to get in trouble, so I never told anyone. It was the worst school year ever.

But even in that, God kept me safe, and he protected my mind because, for many years, I completely forgot about it.

The deception didn't end there. My life would be full of it and eventually I had to decide, enough was enough. I had to wake up to this alarm.

### *Either way, it's painful!*

Sometimes, while learning to accept and circumnavigate life, you learn to camouflage the emotional attachments to your pain. You understand that you cannot change what is happening, but you control how you respond or move forward.

Have you ever slammed your hand on a trunk, a door, or a window? I can hear you now screaming, jumping up and down, or pacing back and forth because of the pain. I bet you'll be more careful next time to make sure the chances of it happening again are slim to none.

Let's connect that example to your heart.

Why do we take our hearts and sit them in the doorways, trunks, window seals, and drawers? Is the need to be loved that deep-rooted that it makes us numb to pain? So numb that the pain tolerance is virtually nonexistent. We walk through life blinded or just too weak to fight to be free. If we truly cared, we would stop slamming our hearts into the door.

Why can I protect those around me, but it seems like protecting my heart is impossible? It's not impossible; initiating it will require some discipline and self-love. What is the cost to save yourself? That's something we just refuse to do. We can give advice to our friends and family, but taking your own advice, well, might actually save your life one day. It's not others we need to save ourselves from; it's OURSELVES we need to save ourselves from. People only do what we allow them to do.

# Chapter 4

## GOING BACK FOR WHAT'S NO LONGER THERE

## ~4~
## GOING BACK FOR WHAT'S NO LONGER THERE

I found it easier to avoid dealing with the problems in my life, so I simply shut down emotionally. I learned to ignore them, thinking that they would eventually burn out and disappear if I consistently avoided addressing them. However, this approach only resulted in me internalizing all my emotions and feelings because nobody seemed to care about my problems. This is a mindset that I developed at a young age; the idea that we should never talk about our issues and just keep them bottled up inside. I never saw my family address any life issues outside of bills, so there was no blueprint to help me navigate or even start a conversation about trauma or concerns of any kind.

You learn to lift the rug with one hand and the broom with the other, then sweep the remnants of your disaster right under it. My mother never told me this was the correct way to deal with circumstances, but she also never told me it wasn't. Many of our behaviors and traits are just learned observations based on our environment.

I learned by observing people that pain is a language that everyone understands. I paid attention to body language, gestures, and eyes. That's when I realized I wasn't alone. There were others who were hurting as much, if not more, than I was. I wondered if they kept their pain bottled up inside just like I did.

I have often heard people say that I don't understand what they are going through or that I haven't been through what they have. However, I want to tell them that they are wrong. Not only do I understand, but I have also lived through similar experiences. I have walked in the same shoes as you and fought the same battles, if not worse. I have similar scars or wounds from the fights that I had to endure. Just because I have done a better job hiding mine doesn't mean they don't exist.

Don't judge me as if I haven't faced any challenges in life yet. I have only started to share my experiences with you, and there are a lot more to come. The only difference is that I chose to heal and not play the victim. I don't always need to share the details of every situation, but in some cases, they can serve as reminders of how far I have come and how much I have grown. It's like climbing a ladder, one step at a time, to get out of the dark place. This approach may work for me, but it might not work for everyone. I have used my pain to help me grow instead of dwelling on it and looking back at old memories.

### *My life was on the line!*

I felt so alone and afraid and cried out to God, questioning how He could leave me in this place with no one to turn to. Day after day, I would cry and ask God how this had happened to me. Remember that man who was with me during my hospital stay? I decided to marry him. Life was not what I thought it would be. Let's take you back to my life in Seattle before the night I woke up being choked by him. The embers were there, but I decided to ignore them and let them create a blaze of fire.

Allow me to take you back to Seattle in September 1997. At the time, I was 21 years old and had been married for two and a half months. When I arrived in Seattle, I had absolutely nothing with me; my belongings had arrived several weeks earlier with my husband. I was traveling with my two-year-old daughter TyAnna, from St. Louis on a Greyhound bus.

I ended up in St. Louis after catching a flight out of Arizona. But wait, I ended up in Arizona after fleeing from San Antonio, Texas, in the middle of the night. Yes, I said fleeing because that is what it felt like! Have you ever been woken up in the middle of the night? For me, it was around 2 AM, and my then-husband was saying, "Wake up, we gotta go! They're watching us from the sky." Precisely, that's what happened to me. We were in such a rush to leave that we grabbed only what we could; some of it being thrown in garbage bags and the rest just in hand. When I went outside my apartment, there was a running U-Haul truck, and the back was already open. So, we just started tossing things in, clothing, books, and other items. We weren't able to take any of our furniture with us. How scary is that? I swear, I still have a picture somewhere of me in a tank top, no bra, shorts, and some flip-flops. That's how I left and hopped in this U-Haul. Thank God my daughter wasn't with us at this time. Could you imagine how hard it would have been to grab a baby and hop in a U-Haul in the middle of the night?

Confusing huh? I can't make this up. My life felt like a hip-hop DJ's turntable, with one album being scratched after the other. We drove from Texas to Arizona, and once we got there, I flew back to St. Louis to celebrate my daughter's second birthday with my family. My, then-husband was supposed to travel the rest of the way to Seattle, where we planned to settle down as a family. I was to join him later. It was a plan we came up with on the fly, and it seemed perfect. I gave him all the money I had, except for the money I needed for a Greyhound bus ticket from St. Louis to Seattle. He was supposed to use the money as a deposit for our new apartment and to pay the first month's rent. However, it turned out to be a bunch of BS.

So, let's fast forward to my arrival in Washington. I arrived in Federal Way, Washington, at about 6 PM on a Sunday. My daughter and I had been on a Greyhound bus for probably 36 hours. All I wanted was a hot bath and to go to bed in our new place, expecting everything to be set up for us, but that was not what I received that evening in Washington. My husband picked us up from the bus station and noticed that we were very hungry, irritated, and extremely tired. He gave us a short tour of the area and then pulled into a storage lot. I was confused as to why we were there. He said he needed to get something. He then looked at me and said he had stored our stuff until we arrived. I looked at him and asked, "If everything is in storage, what will we be sleeping on?" He replied, "Well, I'm sleeping in the car, and there's not enough room for the two of you. And I have to be at work early in the morning."

My heart dropped as I screamed, "What the hell are you talking about? I gave you the $1800 for the place so you could get us settled in!" He just gave me a dumbfounded look as tears started rolling down my face. I felt my knees get weak as I looked down at my two-year-old daughter holding my hand, looking up at me with Mr. Bunny tightly in her left arm. With my mouth wide open, I shook my head in disbelief because we were so tired and hungry. Now homeless in a foreign state.

I cried out, "What am I supposed to do, and why did you allow me to come here with my baby on a 36-hour bus ride if you knew you hadn't done what you were supposed to do?" I was in complete disbelief. The idiot replied nonchalantly, "You've been selling insurance, and your company is huge. I'm sure you can call up contacts up here and stay with them for a few days." I shook my head in disbelief. He continued, "You can always call the shelter because you have a baby, and they will take you fast. Whatever it is, you better think fast because the sun is going down, and I've got to get some sleep. I must be at work super early!"

I picked up my baby girl and took three bags in my right hand and the fourth bag in my left hand. I began walking, crying so hard that I could hardly see. I had no idea what to do. I've never been homeless before. Everything seemed much bigger than normal. The streets had five or six lanes in one direction, as opposed to the two or three lanes I was used to. I was terrified to cross the streets by myself.

I had given him everything, and now I stood with my baby and nothing. I trusted him! I couldn't breathe because I was trying not to cry as I walked, holding this very tired little girl and all these bags. Ty was a smart 2-year-old, and she picked up on everything. She kept lifting her head, shifting her weight to wipe my silent tears, saying, "It's okay, mommy, you don't have to cry!" This made me even more emotional.

I had walked as far as I could and needed to sit down for a minute or two and devise a safety plan for the evening. We stopped at a bus stop a few blocks from the storage unit. I sat Ty and everything on the bench and walked to the pay phone next to the seating area. Don't ask me why I started searching the white pages attached to the booth. It wasn't like I knew anyone there to call for help. That sun was setting fast. I was just thumbing through names and even businesses. I even tried to look for shelters. I called a shelter, and they said they had space, but I would have to be there by 8 PM, and it was already after 7 PM. Another sad truth is that they were in Seattle, and I was in Federal Way. That was the distance of about 45 min to 55 min depending on the highway you hopped on to get there in a car and not a bus.

I fell to the seat at the bus stop, sobbing and crying, gasping for air while watching my daughter squeeze Mr. Bunny tight to her face as if she knew we were in trouble. I looked up to the sky and cried out to GOD! I said, "LORD, please don't leave us here! I don't know what else to do or where else to turn but to you. My daughter and I are tired; we need food and a bath. What do I do, Lord?" I cried, "Please don't leave us here!" And at that exact moment, God lifted my head to see the hotel across the street. I jumped up, grabbing her and our things, thinking, YES, I can make calls from inside their lobby, and at least Ty will be warm and safe.

I walked into the hotel and approached the young man standing at the desk. I told him I had just gotten off a 36-hour Greyhound bus from St. Louis to Seattle and that I had just learned that my daughter and I didn't have a place to go because my husband had stolen the money and abandoned us. I asked if he would be so kind as to allow me to use his phone in the lobby area so I could call around for shelter. He asked me if I had ever stayed in a shelter before. I told the young man that I had never experienced this before. I asked if he was able to direct me to any shelters in the Federal Way area, but he was not able to. He then said, "To be honest, Ma'am, I think the closest shelter is in Seattle." It was then I just broke down and cried and said Lord, what next?

That gentleman's heart must have broken into a million pieces as he looked at me and my daughter, and in his next breath, he extended compassion as God extended grace and mercy to us. He said, "Ma'am, I'm not supposed to do this, but being that we are slow tonight, I will give you a room for you and your daughter. But you have to be gone by checkout." I was so overjoyed! I could hardly speak as I thanked him. I was a mess, tears and snot everywhere. He handed me the key to the room, and I quickly grabbed my baby and started celebrating.

I hurried to the room and started running a bath. Despite not having enough money, I ordered pizza, wings, and soda pop, knowing my check would bounce. I had to feed my daughter, so I ordered more than enough to wrap for her tomorrow. I knew it was wrong, but I had no other option. Desperate times called for desperate measures. While waiting for the pizza, I gave my baby and myself a bath and washed her hair to relax and plan for the morning. I was in survival mode and had to make sure she didn't notice. I was excited when I heard a knock at the door; thinking it was our food. However, it was my husband who pushed past me, saying, good job.

I felt consumed with hatred at that moment, but I didn't say no to him because fear also overwhelmed me. He intruded into the space God had provided for my daughter and me, enjoying the room's warmth, the pizza I had ordered, and even taking a hot bath or shower.

I couldn't sleep that night. I lay next to my daughter, praying and asking God for guidance. As I looked at my hands, which held diamond rings, some gold, and some white gold, I knew I had to find a place to sell them in the morning. This broke my heart, as my mother had given me these pieces of jewelry for birthdays and graduations over the years.

"I had to give them away," I thought. After a sleepless night, I woke up early the next morning to prepare to leave. My husband had already left for work at a rental car place in the airport. I gathered our bags and got my daughter ready. I fed her breakfast and packed our bags while trying to avoid being seen by housekeeping. My only goal was to get enough money to find a safe place to stay that night. I couldn't trust my husband anymore and needed to protect my daughter and myself.

As I reflect on my life, I realize that sometimes I make decisions without consulting God. That's how I ended up in this marriage. I convinced myself that it was better to marry than to live in sin. However, looking back, I realize that my friend Kathy, after the death of my son, warned me not to go to Texas, where my troubles began and eventually led me to be isolated in Seattle.

I can't tell you how many times I've replayed that conversation in my head. At the time, I thought to myself, "Why is this woman of God telling me not to go? This is my chance to start over and even become a wife." But now, I realize she had a message from God that it wasn't the right path for me. I ignored the warning signs and advice she gave me before I left Saint Louis, and now I was in a difficult situation, fighting for my life again. I should have listened, but instead, I thought this was a fresh start.

I felt disgusted with my life. I recall staying at a hotel again after I had sold all of my jewelry. However, I received much less money than I had anticipated. I only got around $200 for eight rings. Despite this, I couldn't refuse the offer. At that moment, I was standing in front of a pawnbroker with my 2-year-old child, feeling desperate and having no money in my pocket. So, even though $200 was far less than what my jewelry was worth, it seemed like $2,000,000 to me.

After leaving the hotel, my partner had an idea to use people's personal information, which he had access to through his job at a car rental company, to rent rooms. I was just happy to have a roof over my head, but I knew it was wrong. I eventually called his mother on a pay phone and asked for help because I was in a tough situation with my daughter and him. She could only afford to send me $100 or $125, but it wasn't enough to help me out.

I remember when I went to that pawn shop, it felt like the longest walk of my life. I had the baby and four bags with me. There was an inn nearby, like a motel, which offered rooms for $25 a night. I noticed how dirty and unkempt it looked as I walked past it. I believe people lived there instead of renting the rooms by the night because there were barbecue grills outside the door and lawn chairs and such. However, I was desperate at this point and suggested this option to my husband. He pointed out that we had no money. I informed him that I had received $125 through Western Union, which I had to go pick up. So, he took me to a local Western Union dealer, and I picked up the money. We then got a room in the motel.

Even now, it brings tears to my eyes to know that I had to resort to this type of lifestyle just to survive. The room was extremely disgusting. When you walked on the floor, it felt like your feet were stuck to the carpet. The room was filled with a heavy smell of smoke. Moreover, when you went to the bathroom area, you could see that the bathtub and the toilet were covered in mold and grim. There was so much mold and dirt in the bathroom that I never took my two-year-old baby girl to use it. Even though she was potty-trained, I had to make her use pull-ups for the time being.

I had to stand over the toilet to pee or poop because I would not put my body on it. No, no, no, don't get me wrong, I tried to clean the toilet. I did my very best, but nothing was cleaning it. There was no way I'd shower or bathe, so I took what my grandma called a duck bath. All of my cleaning happened standing up. How crazy is it that you have to soap your whole body down in the stand-up position in a room that's not the bathroom and rinse off with wet towels? Nope, not the ones that came with the room, either. I had to buy towels.

I was never going to allow my daughter to experience hunger, so I made sure we ate for free every day by calling local fast-food restaurants around lunchtime and telling them that my entire order was messed up during my previous visit. They would offer to fix it and put my name down so I could come back and get a free meal replacement.

I had to find a job quickly because our living conditions weren't sustainable, and even if we could continue to live there, we didn't have enough money to pay the rent after the week ended.

One day, while browsing through the local newspaper, I came across job listings. The advertisement in the paper mentioned they were looking for a building manager or maintenance professional to work on-site, which seemed like a godsend to me. Even though I didn't really want to work as a maintenance or janitor, I was willing to do whatever it took to get out of my current situation.

The offer was to provide services for the largest apartment in the complex in exchange for a place to stay. This apartment was usually rented out for $1900 per month and had an area of approximately 1600 square feet. It felt like I was about to move into a mansion! I contacted the person who had placed the ad and scheduled an interview, informing them that my husband, daughter, and I had just moved from St. Louis and would all be present during the interview as we were temporarily residing in a motel.

We went to the storage and picked out our best clothes. After getting ready, we headed to downtown Seattle, WA, for an interview. The interviewer, Dale, was a friendly country boy who cracked a lot of corny jokes. He explained the job requirements, which involved cleaning apartments after people left. This included repainting portions of the unit, keeping the entire building clean by wiping down, sweeping, and vacuuming, and dusting and cleaning the mailbox area every day using bronze cleaner. We needed to check the trash throughout the building regularly to ensure there were always empty trash cans and clean hallways. Additionally, we may come across occasional maintenance issues, such as a clogged toilet or something that could be handled without requiring a certified professional. I was willing to handle any such tasks. We'd have to sweep up the cigarette butts from in front of the building as well as pick up exterior trash. There was no job too big, small, or disgusting if it allowed me to give my daughter a safe and healthy living environment.

We were lucky enough to get the place and the job, and we were able to move in right away. The apartment was absolutely amazing. My daughter had her own room, the kitchen was beautiful and filled with natural light. There was a long hallway between our room and Ty's room, and there was a washer and dryer in the unit. It was truly a blessing. I promised to take care of the entire building as if it were my own property.

My husband never lifted a finger, yet he enjoyed the benefits of God's abundance in my life. He was a chronic drunk and often would be gone for days at a time. I'm sure he was with other women, but his absence was my blessing. Luckily, my job was great, and it provided enough security to protect my daughter. We lived in downtown Seattle, WA, with the monorail passing straight past our bedroom window. Our location was just four blocks from the Pike Street Market at 5th and Blanchard. I wouldn't complain because I felt blessed.

Although I was very grateful for this opportunity, I knew there was still a need for food in the home, so I took a second job. I became a project manager for Time Life Inc. magazine in downtown Seattle. In addition, I applied for government assistance to help me with food and daycare. I was able to get my daughter into a daycare program pretty quickly.

There were many instances when I searched for a ring or necklace, only to remember that I had lost these items during a difficult time in my life. Even after leaving Seattle, I continued to look for things that were no longer mine. Although I had to give up a lot, I gained a better understanding of who I was by letting go of what didn't matter. Starting anew is simple as long as you're still alive. Unfortunately, some people sacrifice their lives for things that ultimately don't matter.

Seattle was the place of many things. It was where I got to witness God's presence and angels encamping all around me. It was also the place where the real enemy manifested. I had to survive the trauma of domestic violence. I had never had to deal with physical abuse or assault before.

Well, things began to shift quickly. I finally encountered a demon, but I also encountered an Angel who protected me. When the physical abuse started, my life seemed to end. It's a shutdown unlike any other. Living in constant fear. The shallow breaths are taken as you walk on eggshells. Physical abuse in a relationship is a prison sentence. It's a dark hole where, even if you see the light, it's too far off for you to run to. It's like being trapped inside a glass jar with the lid tightly fastened. Do you know that other people see you, but will not attempt to remove the lid to free you? Trust issues become more profound because you no longer have faith and compassion for or in others. You see me but pretend not to, so they don't get involved.

No matter the storm, I always immediately saw God's grace and protection. I thank God that His word said when you train up a child in the way that he or she should go when they get older, they won't depart from it. I promise you, that's my life story because when I'm going through these tough times, my mind always takes me back to Grandma Bea standing in the kitchen, just talking to God. It's almost like I take a quantum leap back to the 80s and watch her talking to God. It prompted me to know what to say to God. I can hear her in one space of my mind saying, "Lord, I know you're able! Lord, I won't be able to do this without you, so I need you to show up!" As she is saying it in one place in my mind, I am saying it in real-time. But in those moments of crying out to God, I found the peace I needed to get me through the storm. My grandmother is long gone, but I am still thanking her for what she put inside of me.

I had a very vivid memory of the tall candle in a glass that had Jesus or praying hands on one side and the other side a prayer. I saw one of those candles in a local Spanish grocery store in Seattle, not far from my home, and I wanted it badly. Lord knows we were so broke we couldn't even pay attention, but I had to get that candle. I also could see my grandmother lighting hers and praying near it. I turned the house upside down to scrape up about three dollars for that candle. I can't express the joy I felt when I brought it home and lit it. I knew in my heart it was inviting the spirit of God to come and be with me.

There have been some pretty dark places in my life. There were some caves and valleys I didn't think I could find my way out of. And even in the darkest of those places, I would find a song in my heart and peace in my mind to keep it moving. Do you know what that's like when your soul is screaming? When your hands are up against the wall, and you're slowly walking through, sliding your feet to the kind of gauge where you are to ensure that you don't trip down a stair or stump your toe. I'm talking about those dark places.

That's the reality of life. You will walk through some situations, and you won't know how to find your way through them. You're going to have to rely on your sense of touch and not your sense of sight.

Have you ever been at home when there is a storm outside, and the lights go out? Because it is your home, you have an idea of where the sofa, table, television, and the bed is so that you don't hurt yourself as you're fumbling your way through the dark period. You've got your hand on the wall, and you're following your way through. You can tell the difference between the living room, hallway, bedroom, and bathroom.

Again, this is going to be your life. There will be situations that will look familiar and feel familiar, and you'll be able to maneuver your way through the dark in many instances. But then there will be times when you're going to be in an environment you've never been in before. If you come into my home and the lights go out, and it's the very first time that you've ever been there, you are not going to be familiar with where to walk, where to step, where to hold onto, and what to watch out for.

I enjoy changing the arrangement of my room twice a month in order to create a different energy flow in the space. However, I must be careful when walking in the dark so as not to trip over anything I've moved. Just like when you trust God, you have to trust your instincts and sense of direction to guide you. Walking with Him requires blind faith, as He is a God that you cannot see, feel, or touch. But when you put your faith in Him, He will guide you by the hand and lead you through those dark places, so you don't get hurt.

---

One day, long ago, while I was rearranging my room, I couldn't find my favorite oversized rug. It was the one I would often lie on while listening to music on the floor.

My mom was always into home decor and believed in changing the feel of a space. We never had to share bedding, rooms, or anything. Her linen closet always had plenty of beautiful curtains, rugs, comforters, bed skirts, and sheet sets.

I went to my mom with a worried face because I wanted to lie on the floor that night and change my rug from a red one to a huge yellow one. I had a special relationship with the oversized yellow rug. Laying there, listening to music, feeling the breeze coming through the tall windows, and experiencing my summer-spring vibe gave me life.

So, I said, "MOM! This is so crazy," she said, "What's crazy BeeBee?" "I can't find my big yellow rug for my floor. I don't know where it is, and I have looked everywhere."

I'll never forget it. Her face looked as if the sun was shining, then it hid behind a cloud when she had to remind me, "You lost it in the FIRE."

I was hurt as I walked away because I forgot. I would never be able to lay on the floor in front of the radio listening to the Quiet Storm again on that rug. Though my room was beautiful and bright, I forgot it was filled with smoke, soot, and char a year earlier. We sometimes forget what we have been through when the current beauty pushes back the sad memory.

Have you ever found yourself searching for something that is no longer there? Maybe you have looked through closets and old bags for something you know you had but can't seem to find. Or maybe you wake up at night reaching out for a lover who used to be there but is no more. It's possible that you have not experienced any of these things. Perhaps your experience is different. Maybe you are suppressing your pain so much that you wake up gasping for breath from what you thought was a dream, but it was actually a memory.

---

I can't recall the exact moment I stopped breathing, but I know that I did. I felt an unbearable pain in my chest and began to take very quick, shallow breaths. At first, I felt a burning sensation in my face, and my nose and throat felt incredibly dry. I opened my eyes quickly, but they filled with water, and I think I blacked out for a moment. It was like an out-of-body experience. I could hear everything as I lay there gasping for my last breath, like a wounded animal.

What just happened? How was I seeing myself lying there? You would think someone would have heard the loud drop to the floor, which, in my mind, sounded like a dresser falling over. But to my surprise, no one came.

Have you ever been at this place in your life, standing in the intersection of lost on the right, broken in front of you, helpless to the left, and pain behind you? Then you drop dead in the middle of this busy exchange, and no one stops to check on you.

It happens! So, this is how we find ourselves walking dead. All you wanted was to check out because there was no connection between living and existing. No one pays attention anyway, so you just wanted out. Yet, I hate to be the bearer of bad news, but you didn't die! Even though you thought it would be so much easier in the past, hurt and pain would die with you. Don't get me wrong, you're in a lot of pain. You're in a battle for life with your heart. You've survived, and you're just having difficulty breathing. It's a lot to take in.

But now I have worse news for you. There's no medical procedure for what just happened. No physician or medicine can make the reality of your pain go away. Easing it will come when you face your truth.

I was trying to not only confront my truth but also discover it. We often hide and guard ourselves so much that we can't even identify our pain, even if it's right in front of us. We would still be searching for it. I knew that something wasn't right in my life. There was a great disconnect within me that only affected me and not those around me. I was everything others needed, but I felt empty when it came to my needs. I didn't even know myself well enough to identify my likes and dislikes. I only knew what others liked; and followed that. That was no way to live. I was living for and with others, but I felt like a stranger to myself.

I started reflecting on my life to understand what was happening. I had a moment of clarity where I saw myself tiptoeing through time, hiding from people, and avoiding the crowd. I was trying to avoid anything my inner critic deemed ugly or unworthy. In my mind, I was holding a beautiful crystal vase filled with hundreds of marbles. I had to be careful not to disturb the marbles while walking because there were too many in the vase. However, something happened, and I'm unsure if I stumbled, tripped, or was startled, but I started losing the marbles from my vase. I was shocked to see all the marbles scattered in different directions on the floor. I tried to keep my eyes on where they were going, but in an urgent attempt to collect as many as I could, I leaned forward and realized that I was losing more marbles as I leaned.

As I stood there in fear, I could not help but watch all the hidden parts of my life being exposed and brought to the surface. My disappointments, rejections, abandonment, abuse, unfulfilled expectations, disloyalty, and untrustworthiness of others are all out in the open now. For the first time in my life, I was truly afraid. I have allowed myself to be vulnerable, exposed, and seen in a light that I was not accustomed to.

I am now okay with being seen as someone who can fall apart and say, "I don't have the answer," "I don't want to talk"; "I don't want to text"; "I don't want to go out"; "I don't want to laugh"; "I don't want to see"; "I don't want to eat." "All I want to do is cry."

We often work hard to hide the secret places of our hearts and fears. We tend to avoid setting aside time to heal, so we continue camouflaging with life accessories.

I just got tired of always being a strong person. I'm naturally an optimistic person and was always there for everyone, but nobody was there for me when I needed it. I didn't want to feel like I had to be strong all the time; it wasn't fair that everyone delegated the task of being Superman to me. One day, I woke up and didn't care what other people thought. I no longer wanted to hide my fears, tears, dreams, and wishes because I was so busy trying to fulfill the wishes and dreams of others. I just wanted to be free in my mind, heart, and spirit. So, the hardest lesson I've learned is recognizing the truth for exactly what it is.

It's alright to revisit old memories as long as you don't get stuck in them and refuse to move forward. Memories can be a collection of both good and bad experiences, so it's important to appreciate what was good and learn from what was bad.

We should understand that the process of healing starts in the mind. Often, we carry unresolved pain within us, which can control our lives like a circuit board. This can lead to a deeper, more profound pain, damaging us at the core and making us believe that we are not good enough.

Sometimes, we cry out for help like a child who has been spanked, but instead of receiving comfort, we are told to stop crying, or else we'll receive further punishment. This phase can be frustrating and hurtful.

# ABOUT THE AUTHOR

I was born Beatrice Corena Bryant in October of 1975. I am a proud mother of four wonderful daughters, each amazing in their own unique way. I am also a grandmother to nine energetic and creative grandchildren, whom I cherish dearly. I am happily married to the most supportive and loving husband, who is not only my best friend but also a major source of strength. He always makes my heart smile and keeps me laughing with his daily jokes. His love has healed many broken places in my heart, and I am eternally grateful to God for blessing me with him.

From a very young age, I was intrigued by the arts, particularly music and writing. By the time I was 16, I recognized my unique gift for connecting with people through song and written communication. My two passions became singing and writing. During the summers, I would spend hours lying on my oversized plush yellow bedroom rug next to my bookshelf that housed my stereo system. I would listen to music for hours, getting lost in the lyrics. Instead of playing outside like other kids, I found myself captivated by the stories within the songs, and I knew I had discovered my gift of communication. So, I wrote and sang, wrote and sang.

As I got older, I began attending spoken word events to test my ability to reach people. The feeling I experienced on stage while sharing my thoughts with the audience transformed my gift. I felt liberated, as if I were no longer trapped in my own mind. I became free on paper, even when my world felt like a cocoon. On stage, I took on the name "Butttafli," and that's how people came to know me.

Although I derive great joy from performing, I never claimed to be a singer, but I will always proclaim that I am a writer.

It took years for me to feel free both on paper and in my life. Eventually, the lid came off the jar, and I embraced my identity as a free "Butttafli." God has said that I would heal people from the inside out! So, I raise my glass to you...Be Free, Be Healed.
~Buttttafli~

www.ingramcontent.com/pod-product-compliance
Lightning Source LLC
Chambersburg PA
CBHW060529100426
42743CB00009B/1469